Saint Mother Theodore Guerin
1798-1856
Foundress of the Sisters of Providence
of Saint Mary-of-the-Woods, Indiana

Mother Theodore Guerin—Saint of God
A Woman For All Time
By Penny Blaker Mitchell

Published by the Office of Congregational Advancement
Sisters of Providence, Saint Mary-of-the-Woods, Indiana 47876

Printed by Jackson Press, Indianapolis, Indiana

Cover Design: Kim Harmless
Photography Coordination: Connie McCammon

Mother Theodore Guerin — Saint of God

A Woman for All Time

Foundress
of the
Sisters of Providence
of Saint Mary-of-the-Woods, Indiana

By Penny Blaker Mitchell

Saint Mary-of-the-Woods, Indiana
2006

Table of Contents

Chapter 10

Chapter 11

Chapter 12

Chapter 13

Chapter 14

Chapter 15

Chapter 16

Introduction

Prepare yourself! You will encounter a warm, lively, holy, human woman in this biography of Saint Mother Theodore Guerin.

I leave you to discover the particulars of her life, her spiritual journey; but I promise you that you will experience a connection with her. Mother Theodore Guerin knew both the gifts and the sorrows of family life; the support of friends as well as misunderstandings with trusted friends; the comfort of her strong faith and moments of darkness and distress.

No matter what the circumstances of life, however, Mother Theodore trusted the Providence of God and loved with deep compassion all persons who entered her life and all of God's created wonders. Her writings and the recorded memories of her contemporaries demonstrate these two qualities in so many touching, humorous and profound ways.

Trust in Providence, loving compassion for all creation—what virtues could be more needed in our day? The best honor we can give our much-loved Mother Theodore is to live as she lived. To do so, we need only begin—now. Each day, begin again. Like her, our trust will deepen and manifest itself to others as hope. Like her, our loving compassion will deepen and manifest itself as Providence for all. May all of us who read her story, model our lives after her life.

I do not want to allow this opportunity to pass without inviting women who may feel the stirrings of desire to live the satisfying and challenging life of a vowed woman religious to initiate a contact with us. Our Congregation, founded by Mother Theodore Guerin, remains vital and vibrant.

In addition, we have a wonderful opportunity for persons drawn by Providence to the charism and mission entrusted to us. Our Providence Associate Relationship allows one to participate in our life and mission.

These and other opportunities to be in relationship with us can be found on our website: www.SistersofPprovidence.org. We invite you to explore and enjoy it!

The Sisters of Providence express our gratitude to Penny Blaker Mitchell both for her creation of the first edition of this biography and for the work she has done to detail the events leading to the October 15, 2006, canonization of this remarkable woman for all times, for all faith traditions.

You may want to get to know more about Mother Theodore by reading her "Journals and Letters," a wonderful compendium of her journals of travel between France and the United States and many of her letters to her sisters, and to priests and bishops, benefactors and friends. This book and many other Saint Mother Theodore Guerin items may be purchased at The Gift Shop at Providence Center at Saint Mary-of-the-Woods or on line at www.provcenter.org.

Sister Denise Wilkinson, SP
General Superior
Saint Mary-of-the-Woods, Indiana
October 2006

Foreword

Imagine...

A woman of middle age, clad in a religious habit of heavy black serge, her delicate face framed in white, sitting in the dancing light of a single candle at a small writing desk of wood. The words she writes are reflected in the emotions that flicker across her face: joy, mirth, thankfulness, determination, bewilderment, sorrow, loneliness, fear.

Imagine ... the same woman walking through a dense forest on a hot summer day. See her pause to watch squirrels playing on the branch of an old sycamore tree. See her admire the red velvet beauty of a cardinal in flight. See her gaze into the cloudless sky as she thanks God for the beauty of the day and of Earth.

See this woman standing in prayerful vigil at the bedside of a child, ill with the dreaded fever of winter.

See her, steady and serene, walking along a weathered wooden dock toward a steamboat. See her, wrapped in a worn black cloak, driving a horse and buggy through the winter rain along a muddy path. See her lingering with another woman over a cup of tea and a biscuit. See her toiling under the hot sun of July as she helps weed the corn and gather the hay.

See her, rosary in hand, standing before a statue of the Madonna, seeking protection and guidance.

See this woman, Mother Theodore Guerin, kneeling in silent prayer before the Holy Eucharist.

Mother Theodore Guerin, a woman for our time, a woman for all time … a woman born more than 200 years ago, who, yet today, touches our hearts and our lives.

Mother Theodore … foundress of the Sisters of Providence of Saint Mary-of-the-Woods, Indiana, superior general, teacher, administrator, businesswoman, farmer, builder, nurse, care giver, daughter, friend, nurturer of hearts and souls, woman of faith, woman of Providence, saint.

Mother Theodore … an ordinary woman who was able to attain extraordinary accomplishments because she loved and trusted God and worked with God to share hope, love, mercy and justice with the people of her day.

Writing this book was, for me, a time of grace. My prayer is that you, too, experience that grace as you come to know Mother Theodore as a friend, a silent companion who inspires you with her faith, who instills the gift of hope in your heart, who tickles you with her gentle sense of humor, who comforts you amidst your trials.

Saint Mother Theodore Guerin, a woman for all time.

Penny Blaker Mitchell

1

Mother Theodore Guerin's Legacy: A Gift for the World

Well, my daughters, ours is a preparation for the generation that will succeed us, and eminent good will be done this way by us. You may not live to see it, but you will have sown the seed, and your sisters will come to reap what will have been sown.

—Mother Theodore Guerin

In the fading light of an October evening, Mother Theodore Guerin, a slight French woman nearing middle age, climbed down from a horse-drawn coach. As her five companion Sisters of Providence cautiously followed, Mother Theodore's dark eyes searched the dense forest, the place where she was to establish a mission. All she saw, standing as she was on the brink of a ravine, were ancient hardwood trees, nearly bare of foliage after days of heavy rain, and rugged earth, covered with soggy slippery leaves and tangled brush.

The priest who had guided the women through the flooded lands west of the Wabash River to Saint Mary-of-the-Woods, Indiana, gestured to a muddy narrow path winding through the forest. Determined not to speak to anyone until they first visited the chapel and the Blessed Sacrament, the women solemnly walked with the priest down the path to a lowly chapel, roughly constructed of logs. There, they knelt in prayer. Later, by the flickering light of a candle, Mother Theodore recorded the moment: "… We went to prostrate ourselves before him to whom we owe our happiness; near Jesus who watched over us with so much love, we could pour out our hearts."

Mother Theodore also wrote of the feelings she experienced when she and her companions, Sisters Olympiade Boyer, St. Vincent Ferrer Gagé, Mary Xavier Lerée, Basilide Sénéschal and Mary Liguori Tiercin, arrived at Saint Mary-of-the-Woods: "What was our astonishment to find ourselves still in the midst of a forest, no village, not even a house in sight. Our guide, having given orders to the driver, led us down into a ravine, whence we beheld through the trees on the other side a frame house with a stable and some sheds. 'There,' he said, 'is the house where the postulants have a room, and where you will lodge until your house is ready.' "

Discouraged but undaunted, Mother Theodore set about the business of establishing a mission. Her charge, as given by her superiors in France and by the bishop of the Diocese of Vincennes, Indiana, was to establish a novitiate, teach the children of pioneer families and minister among the ill and the poor. Less than one year later, in the summer of 1841, Mother Theodore opened the first Sisters of Providence Academy in the United States.

Today, some 166 years later, Mother Theodore's mission continues as the current generation of Sisters of Providence ministers in the United States, the District of Columbia and Asia.

For Sisters of Providence, Mother Theodore remains a source of wisdom and inspiration. At the time of her canonization October 15, 2006, in Rome, the Roman Catholic Church and the Sisters of Providence invited the world to know and honor Mother Theodore as a holy and virtuous woman, a model for all people seeking spiritual meaning, growth and peace.

In this complicated, often perplexing world, Mother Theodore stands strong and steadfast, an ordinary woman whose keen intellect and unwavering faith enabled her to attain extraordinary accomplishments.

While it is true that Mother Theodore lived more than century ago in a world very different from that of today, the challenges, trials, triumphs, joys and sorrows she encountered are ageless.

Many parallels are evident between Mother Theodore's life and our own lives. From the time she was a novice in the Sisters of Providence congregation in Ruillé-sur-Loir, France, Mother Theodore's health was fragile. When she journeyed to the United States, she did not know the English language. Like so many women of today, she knew, from childhood, the shoulder-bending, spirit-numbing responsibilities of feeding, clothing and caring for other people. She experienced the ugliness of prejudice against women and, especially, Catholic women religious. Yet, she willingly sacrificed her personal dreams and ambitions to meet the needs of the people in her life and to respond to the work to which she was called by God and the Church. Direct of manner and determined to follow her religious vows and her conscience, Mother Theodore at times was misunderstood and, occasionally, persecuted. Her life was neither simple nor easy, but she remained generous, loving and just. Through it all, in good times and bad, this holy woman with dark brown eyes and hair and a sweet, gentle face persevered, secure in the knowledge that she was an instrument of God, that she was doing God's work.

A timeless spirituality

Mother Theodore's journey to holiness began when she was a child in the village of Etables, France. She often ran the short distance from her home to the seashore where she climbed atop a high rock or stretched out on the warm sand to watch the dance of the water, to marvel at the wonders of God's world, to talk to God in prayer, and to dream of the day when she could become a nun. Decades later, while she was ministering at Saint Mary-of-the-Woods, Mother Theodore wrote, "What strength the soul draws from prayer! In the midst of a storm, how sweet is the calm it finds in the heart of Jesus. But what comfort is there for those who do not pray?"

Through the years, even during moments of discouragement, Mother Theodore's devotion to God never faltered, for she loved God dearly. She knew that God always was with her, a strong and loyal companion who was by her side and in her heart. As the leader of the mission in Indiana, Mother Theodore frequently reminded Sisters of Providence to nurture their faith and trust in God. She encouraged the sisters: "... rest assured, my dear daughters, if you lean with all your weight upon Providence, you will find yourself well supported."

From the time she received her First Holy Communion at the age of 10, Mother Theodore derived sustenance from the Holy Eucharist. In 1848, while addressing her Congregation of sisters, she described the sacrament as "a daily existing benefit. ... How consoling, my dear daughters, is this mystery of the Holy Eucharist! If we truly knew how to appreciate it, it alone would suffice to fortify and sustain us."

Mother Theodore embraced Mary, the mother of Jesus, with a special devotion. She turned to the Blessed Mother in times of danger and, from the beginning, placed the mission at Saint Mary-of-the-Woods in Mary's care. She attributed the well being of the Sisters of Providence Congregation and its ministries to Mary. She wrote: "We have promised to belong entirely to God. We have made vows, but especially we have invoked Mary and St. Anne, her august mother. It is to them that we owe our preservation."

Generations past and present

As Mother Theodore nurtured her mission in Indiana, she shared her beliefs with Sisters of Providence, students and other people with whom she ministered. Mother Theodore's legacy is woven throughout her instructions to the sisters, in her writings and in the way she expressed her beliefs, the very foundation of her life's actions. All are integral to the Sisters of Providence in their ministries today.

Saint Mary-of-the-Woods is situated along a rugged, forested ridge. To the east, the Wabash River meanders, lazy and serene. The river's flat, sandy bottom lands reach within a couple of miles of the hills of Saint Mary-of-the-Woods. To the north and west, the land flattens and gives way to grain farms and to ragged mounds of soil and deep lakes, the remnants of coal-mining operations.

At Saint Mary-of-the-Woods, the buildings of brick and stone, the Sisters of Providence cemetery, the grottos, shrines and memorials sprawl along the ridge of a hill and beside a ravine, on the brink of which Mother Theodore first stepped in 1840. Many of the buildings, which date back to the turn of the 20th century, are sturdy and solid links with the early history of the Congregation. It is from this place that Sisters of Providence embark to minister to God's people. It is to this place that they return for retreat, spiritual renewal and relaxation and, finally, to spend their last years.

The ministries and programs of the Sisters of Providence are vibrant reflections of Mother Theodore's mission. The Sisters of

Providence Congregation sponsors four institutions devoted to education. Two are located at Saint Mary-of-the-Woods: Saint Mary-of-the-Woods College, the oldest Catholic liberal arts college for women in the United States, is rooted in the original Academy established by Mother Theodore; Woods Day Care/Pre-School cares for children of staff members of the Sisters of Providence and Saint Mary-of-the-Woods College, and for children who live in neighboring communities. Guerin College Preparatory High School (formerly Mother Theodore Guerin High School) is located in River Grove, Illinois; Providence Cristo Rey High School, a new ministry, is situated in center-city Indianapolis, Indiana. The fifth sponsored institution, Providence Health Care, provides health-care services at Saint Mary-of-the-Woods.

Providence Center and White Violet Center for Eco-Justice, sponsored ministries of the Sisters of Providence, also are located at Saint Mary-of-the-Woods.

Providence Center is the home of the National Shrine of Our Lady of Providence, established at Saint Mary-of-the-Woods in 1925 as a devotion to Mary as Our Lady of Providence, Queen of the Home. Programs offered through the National Shrine of Our Lady of Providence encourage family prayer. A series of dioramas depicting the early history of the Sisters of Providence, the Heritage Museum featuring artifacts related to Mother Theodore and other featured exhibits, and the Sisters of Providence Life and Mission photography display depicting the current ministries and programs of the Sisters of Providence also are located at Providence Center.

Through White Violet Center for Eco-Justice, Sisters of Providence seek to care for and preserve Earth's resources. Following the way of Mother Theodore, the Congregation is planting chemical-free gardens and orchards, maintaining a greenhouse, raising alpacas and restoring farmland to its original, natural state. In addition, the Sisters of Providence converted the heating and powering of the motherhouse buildings at Saint Mary-of-the-Woods to biomass, a renewable energy resource derived from byproducts such as agricultural crops, raw materials from the forest and scrap wood from construction projects.

A missionary spirit

From Saint Mary-of-the-Woods, Sisters of Providence go forth with the hope of bringing love, mercy and justice to God's people. Their mission is not unlike that of Mother Theodore, who ventured to the frontier of west-central Indiana with the desire of sharing God's love with the people of the wilderness. So it is that Sisters of Providence today minister in a variety of locations: in schools and parishes in inner cities; among the poor and sick in rural areas of the South; in hospitals and clinics with people who are afflicted with HIV/AIDS, cancer and other life-threatening illnesses; in day-care and retirement facilities for the elderly; at food banks; in Church and Congregation administration; and in traditional and non-traditional classrooms.

Through the years, Sisters of Providence have followed Mother Theodore's tradition of evangelization by ministering wherever they were — and are — needed. The tradition was apparent when the Congregation established schools throughout the United States, opened a hospital and orphanages in Indiana, ministered in military hospitals during the Civil War and in Vietnam, and responded to the need for missionaries in South America. Evangelization is visible today in ministries such as Providence Self Sufficiency Ministries Inc., an incorporated ministry that provides shelter and care for abused and neglected children and strives to enable adults to read, obtain a minimum of a high school education and develop basic life skills.

The Sisters of Providence mission to China, and later to Taiwan, also is reminiscent of Mother Theodore's establishment at Saint Mary-of-the-Woods. Six Sisters of Providence represented the first congregation of women religious from the United States to establish a mission in China. The sisters journeyed to China in November 1920 in response to a request from a bishop who was searching for sisters to open schools for young women in his diocese of Kaifeng in East Honan Province. The sisters provided education for Chinese women; established the Providence Sister Catechists, a community of Chinese women religious; and assisted in developing local parishes. Sisters of Providence remained in China until 1948 when the People's Republic of China, a communist government, began its rule. At that time, the Sisters of Providence and many of the Providence Sister Catechists moved their mission to Taiwan. Today in Taiwan, Sisters of Providence minister in parishes and at Providence University, at Miracle Place, a ministry serving the needs of people who are elderly or home-bound, and at St. Theresa Opportunity Center and Reed School, ministries for children with special needs. .

Sacred reflections

Mother Theodore's faith and holiness are reflected at Saint Mary-of-the-Woods in the Church of the Immaculate Conception, the Blessed Sacrament Chapel and St. Anne Shell Chapel.

From the time of her arrival at Saint Mary-of-the-Woods, Mother Theodore longed to build a beautiful church in honor of Mary, the Mother of Jesus. Though construction of the Church of the Immaculate Conception did not begin until 1886, thirty years after her death, the church remains a beautiful and lasting tribute to Mother Theodore. The church is located at the heart of the motherhouse grounds. Its spire reaches high toward the sky, and its bells chime the hour and beckon all to occasions of worship and celebration.

Throughout her ministry, Mother Theodore encouraged devotion to the Eucharist. Her advice was this: "Send your heart a thousand times a day to adore our Lord really and truly present in the Holy Sacrament." In 1924, the Blessed Sacrament Chapel, located near the Church of the Immaculate Conception, was consecrated as a place of continual prayer and adoration. In this chapel, Sisters of Providence maintain a vigil each day, praying for the needs of the world and for people who request their prayers.

St. Anne Shell Chapel was built in 1844 as an expression of Mother Theodore's devotion to St. Anne. The original structure, built of logs, was replaced by one of stone in 1876. The interior walls are adorned with iridescent shells Sisters of Providence gathered along the Wabash River. Perched on a gentle knoll and shaded by decades-old trees, St. Anne Shell Chapel remains a favorite place for meditation and reflection.

A perpetual legacy

Just beyond the entrance to the Sisters of Providence Cemetery, a Celtic cross, its stone weathered with the storms of ages, stands as a memorial to Mother Theodore. The base of the cross is etched with these words: "I sleep, but my heart watches over this house which I have built."

Mother Theodore died in 1856, only sixteen years after she established the motherhouse and the Academy at Saint Mary-of-the-Woods. Now, all these many generations later, her legacy continues to unfold, a source of comfort, strength, inspiration and hope for all of God's people.

Here then, is Mother Theodore's story...

2

The Beginning

Put yourself gently into the hands of Providence.
Mother Theodore Guerin

A cry — sustained and piercing — echoed through the silence in the little cottage by the sea. Moments later, a baby girl was born.

Isabelle Guérin clutched the baby — swaddled now in a clean, soft cloth — to her breast. The logs in the fireplace toppled and flared, and the tears on Isabelle's face glittered in the golden light. The baby wrapped her tiny fist around one of her mother's fingers, and Isabelle murmured a prayer of thanksgiving and dedicated her newborn daughter, Anne-Thérèse, to Mary, the Blessed Mother of Jesus.

And so it was that Anne-Thérèse Guérin was born October 2, 1798, the feast of the Guardian Angels, in the village of Etables in Brittany, France. Many years later, Anne-Thérèse would be known as Sister St. Theodore and, still later, as Mother

Theodore Guérin, a holy and virtuous woman. For now, though, she is Anne-Thérèse, beloved daughter of Laurent and Isabelle Lefèvre Guérin.

At the time of Anne-Thérèse's birth, the French Revolution was drawing to a close. The eleven years of terror, massacre and destruction devastated France and its people. Churches and schools were closed. Some priests and other Church officials donned disguises to avoid the guillotine. Other priests chose exile as a means of escape; some made their way across the ocean and settled in the United States of America. When the few priests remaining in France celebrated the Eucharist, they did so in secrecy — in dark basements and other hidden, out-of-the-way places.

It was into this world that Anne-Thérèse was born. The family lived a simple life in a cottage not far from the shores of the Atlantic Ocean. Laurent, an officer in the French navy under Napoleon Bonaparte, was away from home most of the time, leaving Isabelle to care for the family. Life was hard for most people of that day, including the Guérin family. Only two of the four children born to Laurent and Isabelle survived to adulthood: Anne-Thérèse and her sister, Marie-Jeanne, who was born in 1803 and died in 1877. Their first born, a son named Jean-Laurent, was born in 1797 and died in 1800, on Anne-Thérèse's second birthday. A second son, Laurent-Marie, lived four years, from 1809 to 1813.

Since the schools were closed, the child Anne-Thérèse was educated by her mother, who taught her reading and catechism. Most of Anne-Thérèse's studies were based on Scripture, providing lessons in Christianity and values that sustained her throughout her life. When she was nine years old, Anne-Thérèse attended a small school in Etables for a short time. Finally, she was taught by a young relative, a former seminarian who lived with the Guérin family for several months.

Even when she was very young, Anne-Thérèse was fascinated by the gray-blue waters of the Atlantic Ocean. Throughout her childhood and on through the years until she left Etables to enter the Sisters of Providence of Ruillé-sur-Loir, Anne-Thérèse passed countless hours praying while she climbed the lofty granite rocks near the shore and walked along the quiet beach. It was here, caressed by the wind and wrapped in the music of the water, that Anne-Thérèse nurtured her love for God and her devotion to Mary and pondered the mysteries revealed in her mother's belief that the ocean was a symbol of eternity.

Anne-Thérèse's spiritual growth was such that she was permitted to receive her First Communion at the age of ten, two years earlier than the norm at the time. On the day of her First Communion, Anne-Thérèse confided to the priest in Etables her desires to give her life to God and to enter a religious community.

Anne-Thérèse was only fifteen when her father was murdered by bandits while he was traveling home to his family. The death of her husband was more than Isabelle could endure. She had experienced the deaths of two sons and many other relatives; Laurent's death left a great void in her life. The intensity of her grief was such that she could barely function. So it was that the responsibility of caring for Isabelle and Marie-Jeanne, and the family's home and garden, immediately fell to Anne-Thérèse. When Marie-Jeanne was old enough to help care for Isabelle, Anne-Thérèse began working as a seamstress to support her family.

Isabelle was incapacitated several years, but all the while Anne-Thérèse harbored her desire to join a religious community. When she was twenty, she asked her mother for permission — and for her blessing — to join a religious order. Isabelle refused. She was a devout woman, but she simply could not imagine losing her precious daughter. Finally, five years later, Isabelle, recognizing the depth of Anne-Thérèse's devotion to God and to her vocation, granted permission for her to follow her heart.

During her hours by the sea, in response to her love of solitude and prayer, Anne-Thérèse contemplated a vocation as a Carmelite sister. As she grew older and witnessed the dire needs of the people of France as they struggled to recover from the Revolution, she decided to share the ministry of the Sisters of Providence, a new congregation devoted to teaching and working among the poor. She planned to minister with the Sisters of Providence ten years before giving the remainder of her life to prayer and contemplation as a Carmelite. As would happen so often in her life, however, Providence intervened and called her to a lifetime of ministry with the Sisters of Providence.

So it was that on August 18, 1823, Anne-Thérèse Guérin entered the Sisters of Providence novitiate at Ruillé, France. She professed first vows September 8, 1825. She professed perpetual vows, which were optional at the time, September 5, 1831. As a Sister of Providence, she was known as Sister St. Theodore.

The Little Providence

The Sisters of Providence of Ruillé-sur-Loir developed from the ministry of Father Jacques-François Dujarié, who desperately wanted to help the people of his parish rise above the chaos and dire poverty left by the French Revolution. Few priests remained in the countryside around Ruillé, and Christian education was not available.

In 1806, Father Dujarié recruited two young women to work among the people of the parish. One of the women served as a teacher while the other visited the sick and poor. As the work progressed, Father Dujarié realized the small society needed a home, but there were no empty cottages in the area, and he was without resources. That did not thwart Father Dujarié's determination. On Sundays, he took the children in his catechism class out to gather stones. Together they wandered the dusty roads and scoured the woods for stones which they piled along the roads. Farmers collected the stones and transported them in wooden carts to the other end of the parish, about three miles from Ruillé. With the stones, Father Dujarié built a small cottage and named it La Petite Providence, or The Little Providence. A two-room structure, La Petite Providence served for several years as school and community room, kitchen and dining area. The dormitory was located in the low and cramped attic.

As more women sought to participate in the charitable works of the little society at La Petite Providence, Father Dujarié began sending them to a neighboring congregation of women religious for basic instruction. During the next several years, the little society grew, and, in 1820, it was organized as a religious congregation. Mother Marie Madeleine (Julie Josephine Zoë) du Roscoät, who entered the community in 1818, was elected to serve as the first superior general of the Sisters of Providence at Ruillé. Father Dujarié drafted a guide for the sisters to follow when professing vows of poverty, chastity and obedience, and added a fourth vow by which they dedicated themselves to teaching young girls and caring for the sick poor.

Shortly after Mother Marie Madeleine was elected superior general, another young woman who was to play a key role in the history of the Sisters of Providence and in the life of Anne-Thérèse Guérin entered the congregation. Aimée Lecor arrived at Ruillé in April of 1820. Six months later, she received the religious habit and the name Sister Cécile. When Mother Marie Madeleine died of typhoid in June of 1822, Sister Cécile was elected superior general. Understanding the congregation's dependence upon Providence and Mary, the Mother of Jesus, she took the name Marie. For the next fifty years, she was known as Mother Mary and is regarded as the co-foundress of the Sisters of Providence at Ruillé. Under her leadership, the congregation grew. A royal decree issued November 19, 1826, approved the congregation and granted it legal existence as a corporation.

The Rule of 1835

From its beginning, the Sisters of Providence congregation functioned under guidelines developed by Father Dujarié but did not have a written Rule, the laws and procedures that direct the life and ministry of members of religious congregations.

In 1834, when the congregation counted 255 professed sisters, Mother Mary asked Monsignor Jean-Baptiste Bouvier, the bishop of Le Mans, to write a Rule. The Rule of 1835, composed by Bishop Bouvier, included one hundred pages of new rules and constitutions. The Rule stated the purpose of the congregation: "… to honor Divine Providence and to second its merciful designs on mankind by devoting themselves to the instruction of young girls and to the care of the unfortunate, whether in their homes, in prisons or in hospitals." Sisters also were expected to contribute to the sanctification of their neighbor, strive for perfection and glorify God. The Rule of 1835 retained the fourth vow created by Father Dujarié. In addition, the Rule stated that each house established by the congregation was to maintain a free school for poor children. The free schools were open after regular classes and offered instruction in sewing and other domestic skills. Sisters also were obligated to maintain a pharmacy at each establishment to dispense remedies, at no charge, to the poor.

The Rule of 1835 placed the Sisters of Providence under the protection of the laws and authority of the bishop of Le Mans, who was to serve as superior for the congregation. The sisters were required to profess vows every five years, but, with the bishop's permission, they had the option of professing perpetual vows.

Early ministries

Anne-Thérèse — now known as Sister St. Theodore — was nearly twenty-five years old when she entered the Sisters of Providence novitiate in August of 1823. Accustomed as she was to obedience, responsibility and sacrifice, she was prepared to assume positions of leadership. Mother Mary was quick to see her talent and potential. In January 1825, while Sister St. Theodore was still a novice, Mother Mary sent her to teach at the Sisters of Providence establishment at Preuilly-sur-Claise.

During her novitiate, Sister St. Theodore was seized with an illness, probably smallpox, that nearly claimed her life. The remedy the physicians administered to her cured the illness but damaged her digestive system. For the remainder of her life, Sister St. Theodore existed on a simple, bland diet that consisted mostly of gruel, liquids and soft foods.

In September of 1825, Sister St. Theodore professed vows and received the religious habit. In 1826, she was named superior of the Sisters of Providence establishment in the parish of St. Aubin at Rennes. Located as it was in a rough-and-tumble section of Rennes, St. Aubin was considered by the Sisters of Providence as the most difficult of their schools. Sister St. Theodore was undaunted by the reputation of the students and approached them with her characteristic grace, charm and love.

Many years later, when she was giving instructions to the Sisters of Providence of Saint Mary-of-the-Woods, Indiana, she recalled her experience at Rennes: "… We must at present be satisfied with the indispensable virtues of a teacher, which are justice and kindness. … You must not think you are guilty of an injustice in rewarding a very restless child when there are others in the class much more quiet. Oh, no! I remember when I was at Rennes having promised rewards to some of my little girls if they were good for only one morning. You must try to invent a means of correcting your children, but remember that the most powerful are rewards; a kind word, an approving glance, a little gesture is sometimes sufficient to correct what the harshest punishments would not have eradicated. It is necessary to be just, that is to say, to have no preference for any child. … But if it is necessary to be just, it is especially necessary to be kind; we must be the mother of our children, have for them maternal attentions and feelings. God confides these young girls to us so that we may form them to virtue. … Speak to them respectfully, and they will respect both you and themselves. Remember that you are the visible Angels to the children and that you ought to conduct yourself toward them as would their holy Guardian Angels…"

Sister St. Theodore ministered at Rennes until 1834. Her expertise as a teacher was such that the behavior and skills of her students and, in turn, of their parents, were transformed. In 1834, Mother St. Charles Jolle, superior general of the Sisters of Providence at Ruillé from 1831 to 1836, sent Sister St. Theodore to serve as superior of a small establishment at Soulaines in the Diocese of Angers.

No record of the reasoning behind the transfer is known to exist. While it was not unusual for sisters to be moved to other establishments every few years, historians frequently express the opinion that the change in ministry resulted from a misunderstanding between Sister St. Theodore and her superiors.

The misunderstanding was rooted in events that occurred many years before. In 1820, when the Sisters of Providence congregation was firmly established, Father Dujarié, at the age of sixty, formed a congregation of brothers. As superior of both congregations, Father Dujarié administered the resources through a common fund, which included his patrimony — money and land he had inherited from his family. Because the Sisters of Providence congregation was recognized as a corporation and, thus, was able to obtain loans, all debts incurred by the brothers were in the name of the Sisters of Providence. Mother Mary feared the brothers' debts eventually would destroy the sisters' congregation. Beginning in 1827, she asked Father Dujarié to separate the two congregations. In 1830, she appealed to the Most Reverend Philippe Carron, then the bishop of Le Mans, who separated the finances of the congregations and appointed Mother Mary, in her role as superior general, to administer the resources of the Sisters of Providence. The congregations were completely separated in 1831.

These were sad years for the Sisters of Providence, for they dearly loved and respected Father Dujarié who was aging, frail and suffering from gout. The emotional turmoil touched everyone. Mother Mary chose not to retain her position, and, in 1831, Sister St. Charles was elected superior general. Sister St. Theodore, who possessed a keen aptitude for business, surely understood the need for the separation. At the same time, she retained her affection for Father Dujarié. Never one to turn from people in need of care, friendship and compassion, Sister St. Theodore spoke with Father Dujarié and sympathized with him. Another sister overheard the conversation and told the superiors, who interpreted Sister St. Theodore's comforting gestures as disloyalty.

Letters written by Bishop Claude-Louis de Lesquen, bishop of the Diocese of Rennes, provide an indication of the suffering Sister St. Theodore experienced as a result of the misunderstanding — and the subsequent transfer. In the end, concerned about the injustice of the situation, the bishop contacted the superiors at Ruillé and succeeded in exonerating Sister St. Theodore of any wrong. In October 1837, he wrote to her: "Sufferings and crosses are wanting to no one, because they enter into the plans of Providence. ... I could quote many others who, instead of becoming distressed or broken up, on the contrary rejoiced that they were judged worthy of being thus nailed to the Cross."

Looking back on Mother Theodore's life, it becomes apparent that the cause of the transfer is of little importance compared to the designs of Providence and the ways in which Sister St. Theodore responded. Sensitive, kind and forgiving, Sister St. Theodore experienced great sorrow. For many years to come, she believed she was in a state of disfavor, or disgrace, with her superiors. Nevertheless, she remained obedient and followed their direction.

The ways of Providence are mysterious. Sorrowing and humiliated, Sister St. Theodore departed for Soulaines to teach and visit the sick poor. There she dedicated herself to the people and the community. She worked alongside a local physician to learn more about medicine and remedies — skills that would enhance her ministry in the years to come. Dismayed to see the church in Soulaines in near ruin, she persuaded Monsieur Perrault de la Bertaudière, one of the town's leading citizens, to finance a new building. As in Rennes, Sister St. Theodore endeared herself to the students and their families and to other people in the community. Her success was such that the inspector for the Academy of Angers awarded her a medal of honor in recognition of her teaching expertise. In Soulaines, too, Sister St. Theodore found time for solitude and the healing grace of prayer.

Called to evangelization

While Sister St. Theodore was in Rennes and Soulaines, events on the other side of the globe were shaping her destiny.

Across the Atlantic Ocean, deep within the heart of the United States of America, an increasing number of homesteaders were settling in Indiana, a raw, new state without schools and with few churches. The need for missionaries to teach the children and to provide spiritual leadership to young and old alike grew each day.

The town of Vincennes, located on the Wabash River in southwestern Indiana, was founded in 1795, but the surge in the state's population did not begin until after 1809 when the Harrison Purchase Treaty opened the way to nearly three million acres of rich land in the northern half of the region. The site of Saint Mary-of-the-Woods, west of the Wabash River and not far from the Illinois state line, is situated on the southern fringe of that land. Across the river, the town of Terre Haute, located about sixty miles north of Vincennes and about five miles southeast of Saint Mary-of-the-Woods, was platted in 1816. The area west of the river remained a wilderness for many years. It was a dense forest of great old oak, walnut, sycamore, beech and elm trees, and, as late as 1820, was populated by only a few hardy individuals.

In 1834, the Most Reverend Simon Gabriel Bruté, a native of France, was named bishop of the thirteenth diocese in the United States, the Diocese of Vincennes, an area that encompassed all of the state of Indiana and the eastern section of Illinois. Bishop Bruté, who began ministering in the state of Maryland in 1810, was fifty-five years old when he was named bishop of Vincennes. His vast diocese was served by one priest, the Reverend Simon Petit Lalumière. Many of the people settling in the diocese were Catholic, of French, Irish and German descent. In 1835, Bishop Bruté sailed to France in search of priests and financial resources. In a report to the Congregation for the Propagation of the Faith, Bishop Bruté stated that his diocese was three hundred and thirty miles long and as many miles wide, with a population of nearly 600,000, about 50,000 of whom were Catholic. Twenty priests and clerics, most from Brittany, responded to his plea for missionaries.

While in Rennes, Bishop Bruté asked Church officials to recommend a priest to minister as his assistant and, eventually, to succeed him. The priest selected for the position was the Reverend Célestine de la Hailandière, a former judge, who was ordained to the priesthood in 1825. After serving ten years in Rennes, Father de la Hailandière was named vicar general of the Diocese of Vincennes. In 1838, the Reverend Stanislaus Buteux was placed in charge of three missions: Terre Haute on the east side of the Wabash River and Thralls and North Arm on the west side of the river near the site Bishop Bruté named Saint Mary-of-the-Woods. Father Buteux lived in a log cabin at Saint Mary-of-the-Woods.

Weakened by the hardships inherent in life and ministry in the wilderness, and suffering from consumption, Bishop Bruté clung to his desire to see sisters ministering in his diocese. In the autumn of 1838, he sent Father de la Hailandière to France to locate a congregation of women religious willing to establish a mission in the diocese. In May of 1839, Father de la Hailandière was named the coadjutor of the Diocese of Vincennes. In June, word of the death of Bishop Bruté reached France, and on August 18, 1839, during a ceremony in Paris, Father de la Hailandière was consecrated bishop of Vincennes.

While in France, Bishop de la Hailandière spoke with the bishops of Rennes and Le Mans and with Mother Mary about the great need for missionary sisters in the United States. After listening to the bishop's plea for assistance, Mother Mary told him the congregation would not make a decision about sending sisters to the Diocese of Vincennes until after the sisters gathered in September for their annual retreat. In September, Mother Mary wrote to the bishop: "We have only one sister capable of making the foundation. If she consents, we shall send you sisters next summer." The sister to whom Mother Mary alluded was Sister St. Theodore.

When the call for volunteers to establish a mission in the United States was announced during the Congregation's annual retreat, Sister St. Theodore did not volunteer. She did not consider herself capable of such a venture, and she feared that her fragile health would hinder the mission. Finally, after long hours of prayer and reflection, and bolstered by words of encouragement from the bishops of Rennes and Le Mans, Sister St. Theodore relented. She would lead the missionary band to Indiana. What else could she do? She feared that the mission would be abandoned if she did not agree to go. And, always obedient, she considered the Rule, which said: "The Congregation being obliged to work with zeal for the sanctification of souls, the sisters will be disposed to go to whatsoever part of the world obedience calls them."

When the Sisters of Providence Council met in August of 1839, Mother Mary told council members that Bishop de la Hailandière could not offer an endowment to support the sisters. The congregation assumed responsibility for the expense of the journey. "Consequently," Mother Mary said, "the sisters will have for their support only the resources of Divine Providence."

In March of 1840, Bishop de la Hailandière wrote to Sister St. Theodore and told her the house that was being built for the sisters would be finished in the summer. He also told her that the little frame church in the village of Saint Mary-of-the-Woods had been destroyed by fire.

Even before arrangements for the mission were complete, Mother Mary, Bishop Bouvier and Bishop de la Hailandière were discussing — via letter — the immediate separation of the new establishment in the United States from the motherhouse at Ruillé. Writing to Bishop Bouvier in April, Bishop de la Hailandière stated, "If you wish, Monsignor, that the house depend solely on me and my successors, I have no serious objection to make. I expressed a contrary wish in the fear that the sisters might be discouraged by the thought of no longer belonging to Ruillé."

In June of 1840, Mother Mary wrote to Sister St. Theodore: "It is decided that you will be the superior of the motherhouse and the superior general of all the other houses that shall be established from it, until such time as the two prelates, the bishop of Le Mans and the bishop of Vincennes, shall otherwise ordain."

Five Sisters of Providence — two professed sisters and three novices — were appointed to accompany Sister St. Theodore to Indiana: Sister St. Vincent Ferrer (Victoire) Gagé, Sister Basilide (Josephine) Sénéschal, Sister Olympiade (Therese) Boyer, Sister Mary Xavier (Frances Louise) Lerée and Sister Mary Liguori (Louise Frances) Tiercin.

After the retreat, Sister St. Theodore returned to Soulaines where she continued her ministry and prepared for the journey to Indiana. In June of 1840, she received a letter from Mother Mary, who wrote: "It is from Ruillé, my dear Theodore, that I bid you goodbye, for it is probable that I shall be deprived of the pleasure of embracing you at your departure, which has been fixed for the fifteenth of next July. ... My hand trembles, my dear Theodore, my heart beats and my tears flow as I write you these words which may be the last I shall say to you. ... God is my witness that I have always loved you from the bottom of my heart, and I will always love you...

"Monsignor cannot, he says, decide anything for the moment with respect to the agreement to be made between Monsignor of Vincennes and him. He wishes that you look over things before concluding anything definitely, because he cannot found his agreement on anything until you are at Vincennes…

"It is agreed that the voyage will be at the expense of Monsignor of Vincennes. He has asked to advance what will be required as far as New York; there you will find money in the keeping of his correspondent, and a priest sent to meet you and direct you on the rest of your journey. … I am leaving for Brittany very tired and very much worried. The life of a superior, my dear daughter, is full of crosses and solicitude. But since victims are required, it is better that they be ourselves than others. We will soon have rest. … Goodbye, my dear Theodore! May the grace and peace of our Lord be with you, everywhere and in all things!"

3

The Providence Journey

*But our hope is in the Providence of God, which has
protected us until the present, and which will provide,
somehow, for our future needs.*

Mother Theodore Guerin

On July 12, 1840, Sister St. Theodore left her Providence home
in Ruillé to begin the first portion of her journey to the United
States. The parting was difficult and very sad, not only for Sister
St. Theodore, but also for the other missionary sisters. They were
leaving behind the other members of the Sisters of Providence
congregation, their families and their beloved homeland to begin
a treacherous voyage across an unpredictable ocean to a land
unknown to them. And, though Mother Mary's absence was
expected, the sisters had hoped she would be present during their
final days at the motherhouse. It was not to be. Mother Mary was
visiting the congregation's establishments in Brittany, an itinerary
developed long before the date of the sisters' departure to the
United States was scheduled by Bishop Bouvier.

On July 25, Sister St. Theodore wrote to Mother Mary to express the sorrow she felt at not being able to see her before leaving France. In the letter, she asked Mother Mary to pardon her and to love the missionary sisters: "Be always our Mother as we will always be your submissive daughters; pray for us, and we, on the abyss of the ocean as in the wilds of America, will invoke heaven in your favor."

Later, Sister St. Theodore wrote of her feelings when the sailing ship *Cincinnati* began moving into the sea: "The moment of separation and of death had come at last. We had to leave all. ... In a word, we bade adieu to all that was dearest to us upon the Earth…"

In quiet moments of solitude, Sister St. Theodore, a gifted and prolific writer, recorded the events of the voyage in a journal and in letters she wrote to Mother Mary and to Bishop Bouvier. Her words illustrate the compassion and deep faith she and her companion sisters shared on sea and on land as they encountered new friends and experiences and as they endured hardship, prejudice, ferocious storms and grave disappointments. It was a lonely, often perplexing journey, as they spoke only French and could not communicate verbally with most of the people they met. Providence was their silent companion.

The crossing

The sisters boarded the *Cincinnati* on Monday, July 27, at Havre. Sister St. Theodore wrote: "The day passed rapidly and brought us to the beginning, in reality, of our exile. We went to the wharf without exchanging a single word with one another, offering in silence our sacrifices to God. Reaching our ship, we ascended with firm steps the narrow plank which was to separate us from the cherished land of France. I passed over first and was immediately followed by my companions. ... It would be difficult to describe what passed in my soul when I felt the vessel beginning to move and I realized that I was no longer in France. It seemed as if my soul were being torn from my body. Finally we left the harbor. … We watched the sails being unfurled one after the other; we saw them swelled by the wind, hurrying us away from our beloved France. … We again offered up to heaven the sacrifice of all that we loved, and we thought of those who were weeping for us…

"On the fifth of August, the wind blew violently from the northeast. In the morning the sea was already troubled, but in the evening, the wind increasing constantly, the waves rose up in a fearful manner and dashed with terrible noise against the sides of the vessel. I cannot describe the majesty which the sea thus raging presents to view — those walls of waves with their foam dashing on all sides, beneath which lies a dark bed. The poor ships, awhile ago so tranquil, were driven about and seemed on the verge of sinking. The waves appeared like mountains that came to bury us in the depths. Our ship, driven by an aft wind, broke through them impetuously and braved them nobly. … We said our Office, but the wind so increased the rolling of the ship that we could neither stand nor kneel down. We became seasick again, and this brought upon me that inflammatory fever which nearly took me to the depths of the ocean…

"We went to bed, but it was not to sleep. The hurricane continued with the same fury in the midst of absolute darkness. The sea lashed our poor ship fearfully; at every instant we thought it would sink. It is a horrible thing to pass the night in the bottom of a vessel, hearing continually the dreadful creaking which makes one fear that it will split open, and that those whose only hope is in it will be engulfed forever. During this time, we prayed to Mary Immaculate; she is the sailors' Star and their great resource. We made the sacrifice of our lives to God, should it please him to require it. … Five days later I was better, though I was not well a single hour at sea. At length the storm ceased and the greatest calm ensued...

"I passed my days contemplating the sea, the clouds, the vessels, the fish ... Once quite a novel scene attracted us from our reverie: a whale of enormous size appeared. It spouted columns of water to an amazing height, and from time to time the monster came toward us; it came, in fact, within a gunshot and exhibited its massive head, which seemed as big as a house. But our proximity was not to its liking, it seemed, for it directed its course elsewhere, lashing its tail with such vigor that had a ship come in its path it would have overturned it."

Always fascinated by other people and the way they encountered life, Sister St. Theodore wrote of the ship's passengers: "... a venerable rabbi who did not think it beneath his dignity to show us a pleasant countenance. ... A poor old woman over seventy years of age, who was always sick, although in appearance less feeble than a person of forty, who seemed well educated, and who owed her salvation, like me, only to the orange flowers given us by the good Countess de Marescot..."

A delightful sense of humor was one of Mother Theodore's special gifts. Her account of the rolling of the *Cincinnati* while traveling with a "good aft wind" at eight knots an hour is one example: "The vessel rolled about like a nut on the sea. When it leaned to the right, it drew our beds and all that was in the room to that side; then, regaining its equilibrium, it threw us with equal violence to the left. Everything aboard shared the same fate. ... In our cabin there might have been seen dishes rolling from one side of the room to go and give a noisy embrace to jars of preserves on the other. The sisters, too, might have been seen falling down as if their legs had been cut off at one stroke. Our dear plump Sister Liguori fell against me with all her weight. I thought I was killed. ... Four times we lighted the candle, but it would not be kept in place. Never did we laugh so heartily as that evening. ... This rocking and rolling had brought us to the Banks of Newfoundland, where we arrived on the twenty-second, twenty-six days after our departure from Havre."

On the twenty-fourth, a great storm rolled across the ocean. "All suffered in body, heart and mind," Sister St. Theodore wrote. "Everything in us seemed to change, except charity, which united us in God. All love one another tenderly, and this consolation is well calculated to support us under the pains we suffer, and also under those which await us."

Physical suffering aside, perhaps the sisters' greatest sorrow was their inability to partake of the Eucharist. "This day was the fifth Sunday that we passed on the ocean," Sister St. Theodore wrote. "The weather was serene and the sea as smooth as a mirror; thus it happened on each successive Sunday, which was quite singular. It would seem that God wished to give us a symbol of the Christian's day of rest by the calm of nature. And, what was most striking was, on Monday the wind would always begin again."

Monday, August 31, was no exception. Sister St. Theodore wrote: "A furious storm arose. The sea was fearful. Almost all our sails were furled. One was nearly carried off, notwithstanding the efforts of the whole crew. Several were torn asunder. The masts were bent like reeds. I had never seen the sea so rough. It was fearfully beautiful.

"...Nothing was heard on board but screams and lamentations. ... While all this was happening below, we were above on the upper deck at our usual places contemplating all that surrounded us, calm and resigned to whatever the Lord might ordain. ... Night having come on, we could no longer remain on deck; we therefore went down to our prayers as usual and, having invoked Mary, Star of the Sea, we went to bed. During the whole night, and the next day, the storm continued.

"The morning of the third day was more calm. We had left the ocean and entered upon the bay leading to New York. ... At dawn the next day, the first object that met our eyes was land!"

In the United States

At 5 p.m., September 4, the *Cincinnati* cast anchor in New York Harbor. Sister St. Theodore wrote, "We threw ourselves on our knees, and with hearts full of gratitude we offered our thanks to God for all the benefits he had bestowed upon us. We prayed to him also for our future; we could not but feel some anxiety about it."

The sisters watched longingly as many of the passengers departed the ship to embrace the friends and relatives who were awaiting them. Arrangements had been made for a representative of Bishop de la Hailandière to meet the sisters when the ship docked at New York, but no one was waiting for them. Soon, however, the sisters found a kind heart in Dr. Sidney A. Doane, who boarded the ship with customs officials. Upon meeting the sisters, he assured them that they, too, soon would be surrounded by friends. Dr. Doane told the sisters he would contact the bishop of New York and tell him of their arrival. Before leaving the ship, he gave the sisters peaches and other food. Sister St. Theodore wrote, "... Scarcely had he vanished than we began to share his gift with our poor traveling companions. The rabbi had given me a fine orange when I was sick. I now gave him one in return and, for interest, added a pear of enormous size..."

The sisters spent the night and the better part of the following day on the ship, secure in the belief that the Providence of God kept them there. Otherwise, they reasoned, where would they have gone? Without a guide, how would they have found a place to sleep? While still on board the ship, Sister St. Theodore wrote to Mother Mary, "… All have considerably changed and grown thin; you would scarcely recognize us. I have been able to take nothing, for the food consists of bacon, ham, salt beef. … The orange flowers for several days were my only food."

At about three in the afternoon, the sisters prepared to step foot on land. Sister St. Theodore wrote: "… we saw a small rowboat coming toward us. Great was our joy in recognizing our captain. He was accompanied by two gentlemen unknown to us; one of them, dressed in black, had a venerable appearance, and I would have taken him for a priest had he worn a cassock; but he was dressed like a secular. He was, however, the Spanish priest, Father Felix Varela, of whom Dr. Doane had spoken, sent by an assistant of Bishop John Hughes out to the bay for us. … He said that we were not to be uneasy about anything, that he had found lodging for us with a French lady where we would be perfectly well received…

"A pretty little green rowboat awaited us at the foot of a ladder, but the sea was frightful. No matter. We had to go. … I whispered to the sisters, "Come, if we have to die, let us die, but say nothing!" With these words I descended first, by the rope ladder, without experiencing the least uneasiness; the others followed, none showing fear except poor Sister Liguori, who was pale and trembling. … Father Varela and two porters had followed with our packages, which amounted to little or nothing, the necessaries for two days; the boat moved off, full as an egg. The rowers battled the waves. … We were rocked as we had never been before, but I paid no attention to this, my eyes being fixed on the vessel we had just left. … Our hearts were heavy. We were leaving those with whom we had suffered. We were leaving our poor ship, which, during forty days, had been our only hope. To leave it was truly painful, so true is it that misfortune binds hearts together."

Father Varela guided the sisters to Brooklyn where they stayed for five days with Sylvia Parmentier, a widow, and her daughters. Mrs. Parmentier was one of many people in New York who saw to the well-being of missionaries when they first arrived in the United States.

"On Monday we had the opportunity of going to confession, and on Tuesday, the feast of the Nativity of the Blessed Virgin, of receiving Communion," Sister St. Theodore wrote. "While shedding an abundance of tears, we renewed that consecration of ourselves to God for the mission to which he had deigned to call us. How sweet for us the moment when we had the happiness of uniting ourselves to Our Lord in the Holy Sacrament, after having been so long deprived of this inestimable favor."

Sister St. Theodore and her companions quickly won the affection of Father Varela, the Parmentier family and Samuel Byerley, a grocer, who made arrangements to have their trunks and boxes shipped to Cincinnati and then on to Vincennes. Mr. Byerley also asked one of his clerks, a gentleman who spoke French, to accompany the sisters to Philadelphia and serve as their interpreter. On September 10, their new friends went with the sisters to board the steamboat that would take them to Philadelphia.

When they arrived in Philadelphia, the sisters were taken to the bishop's residence and then to the house of the Sisters of Charity, where they received word from Bishop de la Hailandière that no one would accompany them to Vincennes. Concerned because they could not speak English, Sister St. Theodore decided not to start for Vincennes without an escort. Later, she wrote, "… Providence again disposed otherwise, and sent us a French priest from Canada, who was himself going to Vincennes, the Reverend William Chartier by name."

The sisters and Father Chartier left Friday, September 18, and traveled by train to Baltimore, where they had dinner in a hotel before going to the house of the Sisters of Charity. The following day they attended Mass at the cathedral and received Holy Communion.

From Baltimore, the sisters traveled by train to Frederick, where they lodged with the Sisters of Charity. Here, the Sisters of Providence were advised to change from their habit into secular dress because of the bigotry and fanaticism they were apt to encounter as they journeyed west. After Mass on Sunday morning, the sisters and Father Chartier climbed into the horse-drawn stagecoach that would take them across the Allegheny Mountains to Wheeling, Virginia — now West Virginia.

Once again Sister St. Theodore was captivated by the beauty of the land: "In this part of the journey every moment unveiled new beauties," she wrote. "At every turn new grandeurs rose before us. Sometimes we were on heights where mountain tops were our footstools ... and in the distance other mountains were superimposed one upon the other so as to form an amphitheatre, where the eye is lost in the ravishing spectacle, so calculated to elevate the soul toward the Author of all things. ... The roadway at times inspired terror also. On one side, vast, jutting rocks would overhang, upon which were giant trees apparently uprooted and ready to fall at any moment; on the other hand, frightful precipices, whose depths one cannot fathom, were ready to swallow us up if our horses made the least false step. This was not the only danger. Bandits infested the mountains, and we had to travel both day and night. But the protecting hand of the Lord, which guarded us on the deep, preserved us from accident and harm on the land."

At Wheeling, the sisters boarded a small steamboat to travel down the Ohio River to Cincinnati. On the boat, twenty-four women were assigned to a room that contained twelve beds.

Later, Sister St. Theodore wrote: "Straw ticks without sheets or pillows were spread on the floor. ... Our situation was not a pleasant one. In the daytime we were obliged to stay in a small space on deck where we were alone, it is true, but where the heat was excessive, not only from the burning sun above us, but from the boiler just below us and a hot pipe nearby."

Four days later, at four in the afternoon of Saturday, September 24, the sisters arrived in Cincinnati, where they encountered an unexpected attack. Once again, Sister St. Theodore's humor comes to play: "We were far from supposing that, in the midst of the city where we had been so well received, we were to find a multitude of enemies athirst for the blood of the French. Until then we had not fought until the shedding of blood, but this was a night of slaughter. I may say without boasting too much that several of my enemies perished by my hands, but I was sorely wounded. All my sisters, except Sister Basilide, bore the glorious scars which proved that they, too, had undergone a bloody battle with the mosquitoes."

Traveling again by steamboat, the sisters ventured to Madison, Indiana, where Bishop de la Hailandière was making a pastoral visit. The bishop, however, had moved on to visit another mission, and the sisters waited two days in an inn before he returned the evening of October 1. Sister St. Theodore remembered, "He gave us his blessing, told us we were to be settled near Terre Haute, and gave as an excuse for not sending for us that his priests were all sick. He conducted us himself to the steamboat and promised to join us at Vincennes in two weeks. ... We left him to go aboard a large boat where we had private rooms and were quite comfortable."

When the steamboat stopped at Louisville, Kentucky, the sisters met Father Stephen Badin, the first priest ordained in the United States. "The next morning, feast of the Angels, he heard our confessions," Sister St. Theodore wrote. "It was a sweet

Sister Rosalie Marie Weller

Born September 7, 1911

Entered Congregation

July 15, 1934

Died February 4, 2015

O Provident God,
hear our prayers for your daughter
who served for 80 years as a Sister
of Providence to bring your gospel
to the world. May she enjoy forever
the heavenly banquet which you
have prepared for your faithful ones.

We ask this through Jesus Christ,
your Son, who lives and reigns
with you and the Holy Spirit, one
God, for ever and ever.

consolation to address ourselves to this venerable priest. It seemed that the words of divine truth had extraordinary strength coming from those lips which had been employed so long in teaching the truth and the faith. He now beholds forty priests in those parts that he alone evangelized for twenty years. ... This holy man, having heard our confessions and encouraging us, said Mass for us. Then he came to take breakfast at the good Sisters of Charity of Nazareth."

Soon the sisters were back on the river traveling toward Evansville, Indiana. Sister St. Theodore wrote: "At Evansville we saw the Ohio River for the last time on Sunday evening, October 4, at the setting of the sun. Nothing troubled the charm and silence of this solitude. Making the most serious reflection on what we beheld, and on our present position, I said to myself: 'Thus does life also pass away, now calm, now agitated, but at last the end is attained. Happy, ah, thrice happy, they who can then look out to the never-ending future with calm and confidence, who can cast themselves on the bosom of God.' ... Naturally I also made reflections about ourselves. We were at the end of our journey by water. ... We were now only fifty-five miles from Vincennes. This was a great joy to us and filled us with gratitude to God, who had protected us in his goodness during this long and perilous voyage."

Shadows

The joy the sisters felt upon nearing their destination was tempered when they encountered Father Anthony Deydier, one of the missionary priests recruited by Bishop Bruté in 1836. "He is under the jurisdiction of the bishop of Vincennes and has evangelized this section of the country," Sister St. Theodore wrote. "So extreme was his poverty and so complete his destitution, that I shall run the risk of being accused of exaggeration in describing it. … The priest is about twenty-eight years of age. His exterior bespoke mildness and he seemed refined; but he was so poorly clothed that one would easily have offered him alms. He had on an old torn coat, shoes in the same condition, trousers all patched up by himself." Delicately, Sister St. Theodore asked about his housekeeper. The priest replied that he did not have a housekeeper. He told Sister St. Theodore, "My companion and I eat only cornbread, which is brought to us every day by a baker. We have only a log hut for our church, house and school. At night we spread a mattress on a bench and there, wrapped in our coverings, we take a little rest. When we are away on missionary duties, and one or the other always is, we sleep on hay or straw or sometimes under a tree."

The sisters were astonished. Sister St. Theodore wrote, "If this narrative, given with the greatest simplicity, saddened us, our hearts were still more oppressed at the sight of the hut which served as a temple to the God of Heaven and Earth and as a habitation for his ministers. With these impressions we got into the stage which was to convey us to Vincennes."

In her journal, Sister St. Theodore described the journey from Evansville to Vincennes on what was known as a corduroy road. "Five minutes later we entered a thick forest where we saw the most singular kind of road that could be imagined. It was formed of logs, of trees that had been felled to clear the way and then were brought together as though to form a raft. Where some of these logs had become rotten, there were large holes. The coach jolted so terribly as to cause large bumps on one's head. This day, indeed, we danced without a fiddle all afternoon…"

Upon reaching Vincennes, the sisters found shelter with the Sisters of Charity of Nazareth, where they ate and changed back into the habit, and then asked to go to the cathedral. "What a cathedral!" Sister St. Theodore wrote. "I could not resist this last shock and wept bitterly, which relieved me somewhat. ... It is a brick building with large windows without curtains; most of the panes of glass are broken; on the roof there is something like the beginning of a steeple, which resembles rather a large chimney fallen into ruins. The interior corresponds perfectly to the exterior: a poor wooden altar, a railing unfinished and yet seemingly decaying with age."

When Bishop de la Hailandière returned to Vincennes, he told Sister St. Theodore her mission would be located in the country a few miles from Terre Haute. "... We consented to start for Terre Haute, and the departure was set for Sunday evening, the eighteenth of October," Sister St. Theodore wrote. The sisters also learned that four postulants were waiting for them at Saint Mary-of-the-Woods and that the chaplain, Father Buteux, was overseeing the construction of their house.

Father Buteux traveled to Vincennes to accompany the Sisters of Providence to Saint Mary-of-the-Woods, but because of storms and rains, the little band did not leave Vincennes until ten o'clock the evening of October 20. Once again, they traveled by stagecoach. Sister St. Theodore wrote: "The night was dark, the roads were very bad. There had been a hard rain for thirty-six hours, which might have made us fear a little deluge. The river, just before almost dry, had now overflowed to such an extent that in several places we could not pass; bridges had been swept away by the torrent; thus, it was not without danger that we were traveling, especially in the night; in fact, we had gone only six miles when the stage was upset in a deep mud hole, throwing us head foremost. When we got up on our feet again, the great trouble was how to get out; for the stages are not open either in front or in the rear, and ours was about five feet wide. ... Having extricated ourselves from the stage, we carried Sister Basilide (who was recovering from a fever) to a little log cabin which, fortunately, was quite near. The man of the house was so kind as to go and help our driver, and we were left to groan at our ease and to warm ourselves in the narrow abode. The woman, about sixty years of age, asked us who we were. As we could not answer except in French, she continued quietly smoking her pipe. ... With much trouble the stage was lifted out of the mud hole and we resumed our journey, but a little distance farther on we had to give it up. We spent the remainder of the night in another farmhouse beside a good fire. ... At daybreak we continued on our way toward Terre Haute, where we arrived in the afternoon without further accident. ... We passed the night there in a hotel, and the next day heard Mass in a small Catholic church — St. Joseph Church, the first parish in Terre Haute — which has just been built."

The final miles

After Mass and breakfast on October 22, the sisters boarded the stage for the short ride to the Wabash River, where they waited until late in the afternoon for a ferry to carry them to the other side.

Sister St. Theodore wrote: "At last we crossed, but scarcely had we been on the road ten minutes than we were again in the forest, and the ground was so covered with water that it was like a vast pond. The plank road having disappeared, it became dangerous to travel on account of trees which had fallen here and there. No matter! The horses were whipped up and they rushed into the water. At every moment we were on the point of being overturned, although Father Buteux went ahead with a pole to sound the road. At length, unable to go any farther, the water being too deep, wet to the skin he had to get up with the driver. ... The water entered the coach and the horses were swimming rather than walking. It was like being in the middle of a sea. ... There was eminent danger for us, and we had two miles to cover in this way.

"I may say, however, that I was not at all alarmed. When one has nothing more to lose, the heart is inaccessible to fear. The water poured in on us. We thought we were surely gone this time; but the driver, without losing his American coolness, managed the horses so dexteriously as to set the carriage up again. We could see dry land a short distance beyond, but the water we had yet to go through was deeper than that we had already passed. The horses, however, were cheered at the sight of land and went into a gallop, the water passing over their backs. There was water in the carriage too. No matter. Five minutes later we were rolling along on *terra firma.*"

*Copy from a daguerreotype of Mother Theodore Guerin
taken in 1855 at Saint Mary-of-the-Woods, Indiana*

(Photo by Sister Catherine Joseph Wilcox)

The ruins of Mother Theodore Guerin's childhood home in Etables-sur-Mer, France

(Photo courtesy of Sisters of Providence Archives)

Abbé Alfred Levitoux and the parishioners at Saint Jean-Baptiste parish in Etables-sur-Mer provided funds for the restoration of the home that was completed in 2002.

Abbé Jacques-François Dujarié, 1767–1838, founder of the Sisters of Providence of Ruillé-sur-Loir, France

Mother Mary Lecor, superior general of the Sisters of Providence at Ruillé-sur-Loir, France, when Anne-Thérèse Guérin entered the congregation

Jean-Baptiste Bouvier, 1783–1854, Bishop of LeMans, France, 1834–1854

The motherhouse of the Sisters of Providence at Ruillé-sur-Loir in France

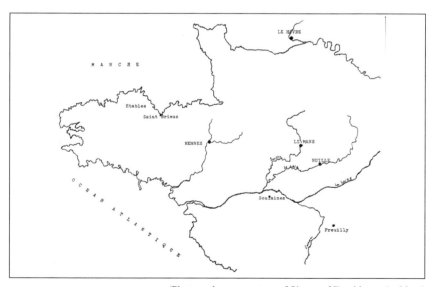

Map of France

By 1811 a small chapel adjoining "Little Providence" had been built in Ruillé-sur-Loir, France. Countess du Roscoat, as Mother Marie Madeline, became the first leader of the congregation. When she left on a business trip, Mother and sisters agreed to keep united by daily reciting the "Prayer of Reunion." Composed by Father Dujarie, this cherished prayer continues to unite Sisters of Providence throughout the world.

(Photo by Connie McCammon)

(Photo courtesy of Sisters of Providence Office of Congregational Advancement)

The scene from dioramas at Saint Mary-of-the-Woods depicts the winter of 1840.

The log chapel at Saint Mary-of-the-Woods in 1840

*The Thralls House served as the first convent
at Saint Mary-of-the-Woods, 1840*

(Drawings by Sister Mary Emmamuel Rinke courtesy of Sisters of Providence Archives)

The Academy at Saint Mary-of-the-Woods

The Providence Convent built by Mother Theodore Guerin

(Drawings courtesy of Sisters of Providence Archives)

Labels on map:

M I C H I G A N

Chicago
Lac Michigan
Notre-Dame
South Bend
Fort Wayne
St Joseph R.
Maumee R.
St Marys R.
Tippecanoe R.
Logansport
Peru
Wabash
I L L I N O I S
I N D I A N A
O H I O
North Arm
St Mary-of-the-Woods
Terre Haute
·Indianapolis
White River
Columbus
Montgomery (St Peter's)
East Fork
North Madison
Madison
Vincennes
Jasper
Jeffersonville
St Francisville
New Albany
Louisville
Lanesville
St Meinrad
Wabash
Evansville
Ohio
K E N T U C K Y

● ETABLISSEMENTS
ouverts par
Mère Théodore Guérin
(1840 - 1855)

(Map courtesy of Sisters of Providence Archives)

*Sisters of Providence establishments and schools in 1856
are indicated on this map of the state of Indiana*

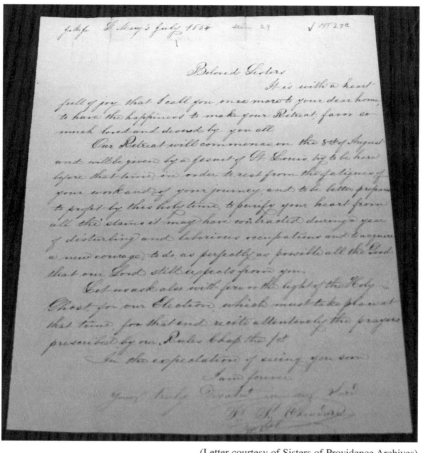

(Letter courtesy of Sisters of Providence Archives)

Mother Theodore Guerin sent this Letter Circular to the Sisters of Providence in July 1854.

Celestine-René-Laurent
Guynemer de la
Hailandière, 1798–1882,
Bishop of Vincennes,
Indiana, 1839–1847

John Stephen Bazin,
1796–1848
Bishop of Vincennes,
1847–1848

James Marie Maurice de
Saint-Palais, 1811–1877,
Bishop of Vincennes,
Indiana, 1849–1877

Father John Corbe,
chaplain at Saint Mary-of-
the-Woods, 1842–1872,
and ecclesiastical superior
of the Sisters of
Providence from 1844
until his death in 1872

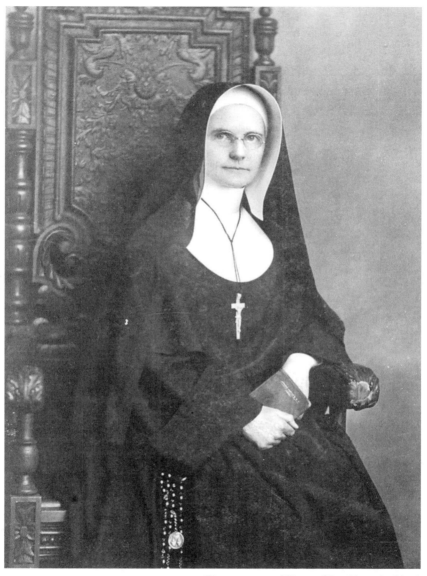

Sister Mary Theodosia Mug was cured of cancer after she prayed at Mother Theodore Guerin's tomb.

On Feb. 1, 1989, the remains of Mother Theodore Guerin were transferred from the crypt to the floor of the Church of the Immaculate Conception near the altar of the Blessed Virgin Mary.

St. Anne Shell Chapel, rebuilt in 1876 to replace the log structure built by Mother Theodore Guerin in 1844

Perrault de la Bertaudière gave this statue of the Madonna to Mother Theodore Guerin and the Sisters of Providence. The Madonna is displayed in the Heritage Museum at Saint Mary-of-the-Woods.

Mother Theodore Guerin's Rosary

The award presented to Mother Theodore (Sister St. Theodore) Guerin by the Academy of Angers, France

(Photos by Katrina D. Thielman)

(Photo courtesy of Sisters of Providence Office of Congregational Advancement)

The Church of the Immaculate Conception at
Saint Mary-of-the-Woods
*The historical marker nearby indicates the location
of the first log cabin chapel.*

A Celtic cross of stone in the Sisters of Providence Cemetery at Saint Mary-of-the-Woods, Indiana, stands as a memorial to Mother Theodore Guerin.

The Sisters of Providence at Ruillé-sur-Loir, France, erected this simple shrine to commemorate the beatification of Mother Theodore Guerin, who entered their congregation in 1823.

(Photo by Katrina D. Thielman)

Crowds of pilgrims filled St. Peter's Square Oct. 25, 1998, when Mother Theodore Guerin was given the title "Blessed" by Pope John Paul II.

(Photo by Katrina D. Thielman)

After the beatification ceremony, the banner of Blessed Mother Theodore Guerin rests upon the facade of St. Peter's Basilica in Rome for the entire world to see (plastic covers the scaffolding erected to make repairs in preparation for the millennium celebration).

(Photo by Katrina D. Thielman)

Sculptor Teresa Clark, in her "studio" in the water plant at Saint Mary-of-the-Woods, created a clay sculpture-model of Mother Theodore Guerin. The statue will be carved from Indiana limestone and will be placed in Mary's Garden at the Basilica of the National Shrine of the Immaculate Conception in Washington, D.C., in the spring of 2007.

(Photo by Pam Lynch)

Philip McCord was cured of a serious eye problem in 2000 after praying at the tomb of Blessed Mother Theodore Guerin.

(Photo by Pam Lynch)

Facilities Management staff members Dave Thomas (left) and Duane Thompson prepare to remove Blessed Mother Theodore's remains from the floor of the church. The remains were placed in a handmade walnut coffin and enshrined October 3, 2006, at the interim shrine in the Church of the Immaculate Conception.

(Photo by Diane Weidenbenner)

Pilgrims file past the interim shrine of Saint Mother Theodore Guerin to venerate her remains and to pray through her intercession.

(Photo by Cheryl Casselman)

Sister Marie Kevin Tighe, Phil McCord and General Superior Sister Denise Wilkinson present a gift to Pope Benedict XVI during the offertory of the Eucharistic Liturgy of canonization.

(Photo by Kim Harmless)

(Left to Right) Sisters Ann Margaret O'Hara, Nancy Nolan and Diane Ris, general superiors during the last years of the Cause for the Beatification and Canonization of Mother Theodore Guerin, place a reliquary with her bone at the shrine near the altar during the canonization ceremony in St. Peter's Square Sunday, October 15, 2006.

Sister Concetta Banez was one of several Sisters of Providence pilgrims who received Holy Communion from Pope Benedict XVI.

Saint Mother Theodore Guerin's canonization was celebrated publicly at Saint Mary-of-the-Woods Sunday, October 22, 2006. This date marks the 166th anniversary of the foundation of the Congregation of the Sisters of Providence at Saint Mary-of-the-Woods.

(Photo by Pam Lynch)

4

The First Years

It is astonishing that this remote solitude has been chosen for a novitiate and especially for an academy. All appearances are against it.

Mother Theodore Guerin

The day was fading into twilight as Sister St. Theodore and her companion Sisters of Providence approached Saint Mary-of-the-Woods.

Sister St. Theodore recorded the moment in her journal: "We continued to advance into the thick woods until suddenly Father Buteux stopped the carriage and said, 'Come down, Sisters, we have arrived.' What was our astonishment to find ourselves still in the midst of the forest, no village, not even a house in sight. Our guide led us down into a ravine, whence we beheld through the trees on the other side a frame house with a stable and some sheds. 'There,' he said, 'is the house where the postulants have a room, and where you will lodge until your house is ready.' "

Having previously agreed to speak to no one until first visiting the church and the Blessed Sacrament, the sisters silently followed Father Buteux along the muddy, winding path to the church. "The church!" Sister St. Theodore wrote. " ... No tabernacle, no altar, for can the name of altar be given to three planks forming a table forty inches long, supported by two stakes driven into the ground? ... A cotton cloth is spread over these planks; there is a small altar stone; and now you have the whole altar. ... This, then, is the church of this place, which is also our chapel. It serves moreover as the dwelling of the priest, and still it is only about thirteen feet wide and fifteen feet long...

"Returning to the moment in which we entered the chapel ... having prayed, wept, and thanked Almighty God for past favors and begged his assistance for the future ... and having placed ourselves under the protection of the Blessed Virgin Mary, we went to embrace the postulants who were awaiting us."

And so it began. The following summer, Sister St. Theodore would open an academy; but for now, though ever gracious and humble, she was bewildered. How would it be possible, she wondered, to establish a novitiate and a school in this remote forest?

The first days

Casting aside her doubts for a moment, Sister St. Theodore and her companion sisters greeted the postulants — Mary Doyle, a Sister of Charity from Vincennes, who on the advice of Bishop de la Hailandière left that community to join the Sisters of Providence; Frances Theriac, a former Sister of Charity of Nazareth of Kentucky; Agnes Dukent and Josephine Pardeillan. They then met the family of Joseph and Sarah Thralls, with whom they were to live until the convent was ready for occupancy.

The sisters' lodging in the Thralls' home consisted of one of the two rooms in the farmhouse and a portion of the attic, or garret. The sisters used their room for baking, dining and recreation. "It is also an infirmary, and this is the only use it serves constantly. We have also a part of the garret, where they had put eight ticks, filled with straw, on the floor. It is so crowded that we have to dress ourselves on the beds and make them up one after the other. This strange dormitory is directly under the roof which is made of shingles badly jointed, thus letting in the wind and rain, making it very cold," Sister St. Theodore wrote.

"…It was, then, in this poor room that we were installed, and here we continue to live in the midst of the forest far from the habitations of men. … Here, too, in an outside kitchen open to the winds, Sister Olympiade makes us soup of bacon and salt beef, except on fast days."

The following morning, the sisters awoke to the brilliant sunshine unique to Indiana in autumn, a blue-crystal sky and a brisk breeze. Venturing into the woods, they located the tiny log chapel, where they knelt in prayer before the Blessed Sacrament. Thus sustained and filled with hope, the sisters sought a glimpse of the building that was being constructed for them. "Like the castles of the knights of old, it is so deeply hidden in the woods that one cannot see it until she comes up to it," Sister St. Theodore wrote. "It is a pretty two-story brick house, fifty feet wide by twenty-six feet deep. There are five large openings in front. The first stone was laid August 17, and it is already roofed. Today they began plastering, but there are yet neither doors nor windows; all is being done, little by little. As to our garden and yard, we have all the woods. And the wilderness is our only cloister, for our house is like an oak tree planted therein."

In the days that followed, the sisters explored the woods and soon discovered the abundance of medicinal plants, herbs, fruits — wild grapes, persimmons and pawpaws — nuts and berries waiting for harvest. Sister St. Theodore surveyed the land and began considering ways to employ Thomas Brassier and his family, for they were expected to arrive within the next few days. Sister St. Theodore met the Brassiers during the voyage from France to the United States and invited them to work at Saint Mary-of-the-Woods. "The man is to clear a corner of our land where cabbage and other vegetables will be planted next spring if we do not freeze before that time; for they say that the winter here is unbearable. Every year several persons are frozen to death," Sister St. Theodore wrote.

"It is astonishing that this remote solitude has been chosen for a novitiate and especially for an academy. All appearances are against it. I have given my opinion frankly to the bishop, to Father Buteux, and, in fine, to all who have any interest in the success of our work. All have given reasons that are not entirely satisfactory; yet I dare not disregard them. The spirit of this country is so different from ours that one would have to be familiar with it before condemning those who know it better than we do. I await the issue, then, before passing a definite judgment. ... If we cannot do any good here, you know our agreement, we will return to our own country. ... Without the aid of France, what would become of the poor missionaries who, notwithstanding, are so miserable? What would become of us also? It was a Frenchman, Joseph Picquet of Sainte Marie, Illinois, who gave the money to build our house. Who will now support it? Oh! The Daughters of Providence must fear nothing as to their future. They must confide themselves entirely to their good Mother, the Blessed Virgin Mary."

The French sisters immediately began studying the English language, and Sister St. Theodore began instructing the postulants about the ways of religious life. In addition, Sister St. Theodore had crucial concerns to address. It was obvious that the house would not be finished before the start of winter; where would they live? Her funds were nearly depleted; how would she finance the mission?

Her solution was quick: the farmhouse, if Mr. Thralls was willing to sell it, would serve as a convent, while the building under construction would be used as a school, thus providing an income for the Congregation. Within days, she composed the plan and presented it to Bishop de la Hailandière, who recognized the wisdom of it. When the bishop visited Saint Mary-of-the-Woods in November, he purchased the Thralls' farm, domestic animals and equipment for eighteen hundred dollars. The Sisters of Providence contributed two hundred dollars toward the purchase of the house, which was destined to serve as the Congregation's motherhouse for thirteen years. The Thralls family moved to another homestead a couple of miles away.

Sister St. Theodore recorded the transaction in her journal: "The twenty-seventh of November we were in possession of this farm, Mr. Thralls having left with his family." The following day, the sisters prepared an altar in one of the rooms of the farmhouse. On November 29, Sister St. Theodore wrote, "We have the happiness of preserving the Blessed Sacrament. … This same day, which was the first Sunday of Advent, we began a retreat which was given us by Father Augustine Martin," a missionary priest who served as vicar general for Bishop de la Hailandière.

Writing to Mother Mary, Sister St. Theodore explained the transaction: "To prove his good will, Monsignor has just bought us two tilled fields and a little orchard quite near the house they are building for us; but as the most pressing concern for us was a lodging for the winter, we have bought the house where we are, which is, as I have already told you, a little farm house, the only one of the kind I have seen in this country. This house, which is in reality only a cabin, will cost four hundred dollars gold. I still had the thousand francs … I thought I could not do better than to give them, for otherwise we would have had neither house, nor field, nor orchard. You will blame me, perhaps, Mother, and will say I have been too hasty. If you had been here and had understood our situation, I do not think you would pass the same judgment. It was impossible to spend the winter, which is already very cold, and will become colder, in a cabin open to all the winds, having neither doors not windows that close. Repairs were necessary, and could not be carried out, for we were mixed in with the farmers and their children in a manner not only annoying, but unsuitable. Now at least, however badly situated, we are by ourselves. We can fulfill our Rule and we shall have the inestimable advantage of having the Blessed Sacrament in our dwelling. It will help us to suffer and to die if we must. With Jesus, what shall we have to fear?"

Shortly after the sisters arrived at Saint Mary-of-the-Woods, Bishop de la Hailandière told Sister St. Theodore to ask the sisters to address her as "Mère" — the French word for "mother." For all of the Sisters of Providence from France, that title was reserved — in their hearts — for one woman, Mother Mary Lecor.

So, instead, Sister St. Theodore asked the sisters to address her as "Mother," a title she would bear the remainder of her life.

Mother Theodore's illness

Bishop de la Hailandière returned to Saint Mary-of-the-Woods on December 23 and stayed to preside at Midnight Mass on

Christmas Eve. On Christmas night, Mother Theodore began suffering with fever, severe headaches and periods of unconsciousness, an illness a physician from Vincennes eventually diagnosed as "brain fever." The bishop, the sisters and the physician feared she would die. While Mother Theodore was ill, Bishop de la Hailandière wrote to Father Martin, "… My reverend Mother Theodore has just been ill unto death; I believe her to be almost out of danger now, but what uneasiness her condition caused us! For my part, I consider it a real miracle that she is still breathing. I spent many nights at her bedside. Poor daughter, how much she suffered, and with what patience! I now have her confidence, and I can say that she has given it to me without limits."

The illness lingered into mid-February, when Mother Theodore was finally strong enough to visit the chapel and receive the Eucharist. As soon as she recovered, Mother Theodore began supervising the spring planting of potatoes and other vegetables and preparing for the opening of the school. The spring planting was vital to the sisters' survival through another harsh winter. The Brassiers planted corn and wheat which necessitated the purchase of plows and other equipment, along with a horse named Mignon. Mother Theodore also saw to the planting of additional fruit-bearing trees in the small orchard already growing on the farm.

The Academy

Public education was only just beginning in the United States in 1840 and, at that, was limited to cities in the East. In Indiana, reading, writing and arithmetic were taught at the few one-room schools scattered across the state. Mother Theodore modeled the Academy at Saint Mary-of-the-Woods after the one at Ruillé and dedicated it to the protection of Mary, the Mother of Jesus. She prepared a prospectus and announced the opening of the school in the June 19, 1841, edition of the Wabash Courier, the newspaper published in Terre Haute at the time. The announcement stated: "St. Mary's Academy for Young Ladies will open the second of July. Branches taught are as follows: Reading, Writing, Arithmetic, Geography and History, both Ancient and Modern, English Composition, Natural Philosophy, Chemistry, Botany, Mythology, Biography, Astronomy, Rhetoric, Plain and Fancy Needlework, Bead Work, Tapestry, and Lace Work.

"Terms — Boarding, including the above branches, per annum, $100.

"Extra charges: French language, per annum, $10; Music, instrumental and vocal, $30; Drawing and painting in water colors, imitation of oil paintings on linen, $20; Oil painting on velvet, oriental painting, embroidery and artificial flower work, $10; Washing and mending per annum, $12; Stationery, $5; Medicine at apothecaries' rate.

"Those who wish to learn the Latin, German and Italian languages can do so. Terms the same as for the French. For further particulars, application must be made to the Mother Superior. All letters directed to the Institution must be postpaid. — Mother Theodore."

The first student, whose name was Mary, arrived at Saint Mary-of-the-Woods on July 4, 1841. Two other young women arrived the following day, and by the end of the month the school counted ten students. The first session ended in August, with classes scheduled to resume in September after the Sisters of Providence retreat.

In her "Reminiscences," Mother Anastasie Brown, one of the first pupils of the Academy and, many years later, the superior general of the Congregation, said:

"…I remember visiting the new convent one Sunday in company with my father, who was already acquainted with Mother Theodore owing to his having furnished the brick for the new Academy. … When Mother Theodore came to meet us, I was at once completely won by her amiable manners. She manifested an exquisitely simple cordiality, but when occasion required, she could be a queen in dignity. Knowing of my desire to be a religious, she took me at once to her heart in a way the memory of which is today one of my dearest treasures…

"Some time after the Academy opened in September 1841, my sister and I entered as pupils; our arrival raised the number of students to thirteen. Sister Basilide had succeeded Sister St. Vincent as superior; she also taught nearly all the classes except English which was in charge of the first Sister Ann Joseph, an American novice, and catechism given by Sister St. Francis, who also taught drawing. Mother Theodore gave instructions from time to time and took the greatest personal interest in all the classes, especially the mathematics."

New establishments

The missionary priests welcomed the sisters to Indiana and almost immediately began asking them to open schools in their communities. In 1840, of the more than 250,000 children in Indiana, fewer than 50,000 regularly attended school. At least one-seventh of the adult population could neither read nor write.

While Mother Theodore recognized the great need for schools and teachers, her zeal was tempered by a bone-deep knowledge that sisters sent to establish schools should, themselves, first be well educated and prepared for the responsibility.

In 1841, Mother Theodore promised Father Joseph Kundek that she would send sisters for a school in Jasper, Indiana, a small, but growing German community located júst a few miles from the old Buffalo Trace in southern Indiana. The people of Jasper made the bricks with which to build a church and a house for the sisters. The school opened on the feast of St. Joseph, March 19, 1842. Sister Marie Joseph (Yvonne) Pardeillan, who spoke German, and Sister Gabriella Moore were sent to the school to teach the fifty boys and girls who were enrolled. Sister St. Vincent was the superior.

Later that spring, Mother Theodore opened a free school, called Nazareth, for the children who lived in and near the village of Saint Mary-of-the-Woods.

In October of 1842, Mother Theodore installed Sister St. Liguori and Sister Augustine in a log cabin school at St. Francisville, Illinois, a settlement of Canadians and Americans located twelve miles from Vincennes. Father Louis Ducoudray, who was a cousin of Bishop de la Hailandière, was without resources, so he gave his house for the school, which had an enrollment of about sixty children.

New arrivals

In November 1841, Sister St. Francis Xavier (Irma) Le Fer de la Motte and Sister Mary Cecilia (Eleanor Kinzie) Bailly, both of whom were destined for vital roles in the Congregation, arrived at Saint Mary-of-the-Woods.

Bishop de la Hailandière first met Sister St. Francis Xavier in France in 1839. He had hoped that she would accompany the missionary band of sisters to Indiana, but Mother Mary insisted she remain in France for additional instruction. Sister St. Francis Xavier was a woman of virtue and intelligence, and she and Mother Theodore became close friends. Sister St. Francis Xavier helped in the novitiate, taught catechism to the children in the village of Saint Mary-of-the-Woods, and taught drawing and painting at the boarding school.

Sister Mary Cecilia was elected superior general of the Congregation after the death of Mother Theodore in 1856. The daughter of a Canadian fur trader and an American Indian princess, Sister Mary Cecilia was educated in Detroit and Montreal. She spoke French and English.

Trials

A disquieting anxiety permeated all of the sisters' activities during those early months at Saint Mary-of-the-Woods. Mother Theodore and the sisters who accompanied her from France feared that their fledgling mission would be separated from the motherhouse in Ruillé. Mother Theodore expressed that fear in nearly every letter she wrote to Mother Mary and to Bishop Bouvier.

Months passed into years, yet the question of who was responsible for the Sisters of Providence of Saint Mary-of-the-Woods remained unanswered. The sisters received little financial assistance from the motherhouse in Ruillé or from the Diocese of Vincennes. Bishop de la Hailandière had a meager amount of money with which to support the priests and sisters in his vast diocese. Mother Mary needed all of her resources to maintain and expand ministries in France.

In the meantime, Mother Theodore nurtured and protected the little mission and the sisters, and struggled to preserve the integrity of the Sisters of Providence Rule and Constitutions. Her dedication to the Rule frequently conflicted with the wishes of Bishop de la Hailandière. She turned, oh so often, to Mother Mary for guidance and support, but communication was limited to correspondence, and that, in itself, posed another complication. Four to eight weeks or more passed before letters sent from Saint Mary-of-the-Woods reached Ruillé. Time and trouble did not wait for replies. All things considered — including the fact that Mother Theodore, Mother Mary and Bishop de la Hailandière were all strong-willed, zealous individuals — misunderstandings were, perhaps, inevitable.

Letters written by Bishop de la Hailandière show beyond a doubt that he respected Mother Theodore and was fond of her. Still, his personality was such that he tended to rule rather than guide. At the time of Mother Theodore's illness, the bishop wrote to Mother Mary: "However great our hopes, however, I must confess to you that they would vanish like smoke if Sister Theodore were taken away from us. In fact, she leaves nothing to be desired, either in qualities of heart and mind, or in the virtues that one desires to see in a superior and foundress. …"

Mother Theodore regarded Bishop de la Hailandière with the respect and honor accorded a bishop. She described him as "… an excellent father. I have never found a heart more compassionate, more charitable, under an exterior so cold. … He seems animated by the best intentions, but he is so busy, so poor, that truly he knows not what to do. … With me he appears very reserved, telling me only what he cannot avoid, but again I may be the cause of it by the resolute tone I took when it was a question of costume or of going into the country…"

Writing to Bishop Bouvier, Mother Theodore openly expressed her growing concerns about her relationship with Bishop de la Hailandière and the future of the Sisters of Providence of Saint Mary-of-the-Woods. She wrote: "I am not always in agreement with this good superior; for the reception of subjects, admission to the habit, and even to the vows, and the undertaking of establishments; I am afraid of going too fast, and Monsignor says that in this country nothing is done slowly. … We fear a little for the future. … My request for a favor that

I ask of you in the name of all your daughters of the forest, French as well as American: it is that you never permit that this poor little house of the desert be separated from its trunk; if you cut it off it will wither like the branch cut from the trunk which gave it life."

At times, it seemed that Mother Theodore could please no one. After reading Mother Theodore's journal accounts of the voyage, Mother Mary wrote: "We have read your little account of the voyage, with interest, but to be frank with you, from afar as from near at hand, we would have preferred it if you had written in a style less romantic and more pious. ... Finally, it is difficult for us to judge from here what would be for the best there, but we are confident that you will be able to get along when you have sufficient knowledge of the country in which you are living."

When Mother Theodore told Mother Mary that the bishop wished her to be called Mother, she replied: "... Although you bear the name of Mother, my dear Theodore, do not forget that you belong still to the Providence of Ruillé. ..."

During that first winter and spring at Saint Mary-of-the-Woods, Mother Theodore continued to doubt her ability to lead the little Congregation. She wrote to Mother Mary: "I represented to you what you already knew better than I, that I was not capable of so sublime and sacred a work. Many times I expressed to you my fears in all this regard, but when you wrote that, in spite of my representations and all my objections, it was decided that I should go to America, oh, then, of my own free will, I embraced this dear mission with all the ardor of my heart, and I esteemed it the greatest grace I have ever received from God to be chosen among so many others, infinitely more capable, to bring it to success. ... I am persuaded that my vocation is limited to bringing the sisters to Vincennes. They are here; my task is fulfilled, and to abler and especially to holier hands is it reserved to found here a Congregation of missionary sisters. My duty has been simply that of the ass who bore the prophet."

Mother Theodore's feelings were reinforced by Father Buteux, the Congregation's chaplain, who believed he had authority over all aspects of the community. Like Bishop de la Hailandière, he thought the director of the school should be a person familiar with American ways and customs, and favored Sister Aloysia, a novice, for the position. His influence on Mother Theodore was such that she began fearing her presence would harm the mission, and, for a time, she considered leaving — an action Bishop de la Hailandière forbade.

In August of 1841, acting on the advice of Father Martin and Father Benjamin Petit, in whom Mother Theodore had confided, Bishop de la Hailandière withdrew Father Buteux as chaplain of the Sisters of Providence.

Writing to Mother Mary, Mother Theodore recounted that event: "... another vexation, and one that has done us more injury, was the want of judgment in our poor chaplain, Father Buteux, who, it seems to me at least, with a good intention has done considerable harm especially in regard to myself. He had dreams of a religious house according to his own ideas ... and he would change all our Rules ... This worthy man, seeing that I was a wrench in the works, tried to convince Monsignor that I was not suitable for the position in which I was placed, and that the most essential qualifications were wanting in me. ... Then he took another course, that of making me believe myself that I would do a great wrong to the house through the extreme differences of my character from the Americans."

The trouble did not end with the removal of the priest as chaplain for the convent. Mother Theodore wrote: "Father Buteux himself, contrary to the prohibition that he received, continued to see the sisters of the boarding school, and even to write to Sister Aloysia without my knowing it; the subject was the founding of a community according to his original plan, making his protégé the superior, whether of our house or of another. Proud of his patronage, the sister had herself spoken to four of the postulants and had them spoken to, to engage them to follow her in the spring. ... When all these plots were discovered, I took our little buggy and set out for Vincennes on the nineteenth of January, in spite of the cold and the thickly falling snow. I was wrapped up in an old buffalo skin and, sheltered by an umbrella, I arrived at the bishop's house at nine o'clock that night. ... His lordship ended by promising to come and send away the unworthy subject who had already given us so much trouble."

Bishop de la Hailandière arrived at Saint Mary-of-the-Woods a few days later and assembled a Council which included Mother Theodore, Sister St. Vincent, Sister Basilide and Sister St. Francis Xavier to examine the conduct of Sister Aloysia. The Council decided to dismiss Sister Aloysia from the Sisters of Providence Congregation.

Mary Doyle (Sister Aloysia) relocated in Terre Haute, where she lived with a Catholic woman and attempted to open a school. The school did not succeed, but its creation and the rumors surrounding it were sources of grief and distress for the Sisters of Providence. The situation awakened prejudice among the people of Terre Haute, causing them to distrust the Sisters of Providence. Enrollment in the Academy at Saint Mary-of-the-Woods dropped sharply, and shopkeepers in Terre Haute began denying credit to the Sisters of Providence, who were nearly without resources.

While all of these events were unfolding in Indiana, Mother Mary received an anonymous letter which presented a disturbing and inaccurate account of life at Saint Mary-of-the-Woods. Writing to Mother Theodore in December of 1841,

Mother Mary said: "A person who is entirely unknown to me and who seems to have a great interest in our Congregation and to be prompted to the action he takes only by a motive of charity, writes to us from Cincinnati that the six sisters we have sent to Vincennes are in great difficulties and are suffering much; that the superior, Sister Theodore, does not inform us, for motives unknown, and that it is in order to supply for this reserve on your part that the kind stranger ventures to write a few lines…"

Mother Mary continued: "I order you, without consulting anyone but the obedience you owe us, to inform us of all that concerns you, both in general and in particular. I want to know everything, my dear Theodore. … On what do you live? Do you plant wheat? Do you make butter? And have you any milk? It is no use to ask you; you always tell me nothing." The identity of the letter writer was never determined, but the letter was a source of heartache for Mother Theodore who already was nearly overwhelmed by feelings of inadequacy.

When Mother Theodore received Mother Mary's letter late in February of 1842, she responded immediately. "It is true that our life on the whole is a life of sacrifice. Can it be doubted? Strangers to the manners, the customs, the religious views, and especially to the character of those who surround us; thrown into the depths of the vast forest of Indiana … our life is hard; obliged to have business relations with a people whose language we do not understand, a people noted for its skill in and inclination toward sharp dealing, having in our own house Americans … certainly is like killing us, so to speak, with pinpricks. … You knew all that so well that you told it all to me yourself before I came to this country."

In an attempt to assure Mother Mary that the situation was not as desperate as the anonymous letter writer indicated, Mother Theodore described the way of life for the Sisters of Providence of Saint Mary-of-the-Woods: "We have a little chapel where we possess the happiness of having the Blessed Sacrament. We have Holy Mass every day and Benediction twice a week. This chapel, made of an enclosed porch and only seven feet high, is quite respectable. We whitewashed and painted it ourselves. It contains a beautiful statue of the Blessed Virgin, which was sent by Perrault de la Bertaudière, with candlesticks and a fine silver-plated crucifix.

"Our house is composed of three parts: one room which serves every purpose and which we use for common assembly; another (called mine) in which we take our recreations, study our English lessons, hold Chapter, and also hold Council meetings; lastly, there is a dormitory containing fifteen beds that completely fill it. The bishop has had us build two wings to this house. They are now under roof, and in the spring we shall have their doors and windows put in. Then we shall be fairly well lodged for daughters of the forest. Our boarding school is a brick house, very suitable and even too pretty for sisters…

"We have three horses and a little colt, two oxen, six calves, perhaps fifty or sixty hogs, eight turkeys, maybe more than a hundred chickens, some geese, five sheep and a tiny lamb. … Our men are busy all winter cutting wood, and yet they can scarcely supply our three houses including the priest's house.

"We are well provided with wheat bread. We can have wheat flour of the best quality at two dollars and a half the hundredweight. … Good beef is two cents; pork, two cents; butter, eight, nine and ten cents, sometimes twelve cents in the depths of winter. … Eggs are five cents a dozen. Everything is delivered to us. … We sleep on folding beds with feather ticks, for wool and horsehair are very dear. We have made foot coverlets of cotton batting that costs twenty cents a pound.

"In Lent we have only two days of abstinence a week,

Wednesday and Friday. It is permitted to take a cup of coffee in the morning with a morsel of bread about the size of an egg. That is called fasting, and of course it is, since the Church permits it. ... Truly, a good spirit reigns in our house. ... At least, my dear Mother, pray for me. O, what great need I have of the help of Heaven! What will become of the souls of my very dear sisters, if I do not lead them to God!"

Mother Theodore's trials were not at an end. The question of whether the mission would be separated from the motherhouse in Ruillé remained unanswered, a constant source of apprehension. Her friend, Father Napoleon Perché of New Orleans, offered advice: "... you would do well to write to your superiors in France, and have them give you the orders for all that you believe useful for the success of your work. You must tell them in detail what it is you believe they should command you; and these orders, coming from persons whom you are bound to obey, will deliver you from the difficulties that the bishop or others might arouse. ... It is necessary to remain firm, my dear daughter. You know very well that we must 'suffer persecutions for justice'; that is the way by which all the saints have passed. I know that the hardest trials are those which come to us from persons for whom we have esteem and respect. But I know you so well, my very dear daughter, that I am convinced that in the accomplishment of your duties you will draw back from no trial, whatever it may be."

In August of 1842, Mother Theodore wrote to Mother St. Charles: "It seems to me, and I have always felt, that the fate of our little house of the forest is in your hands; if you protect it, it will succeed; but if you abandon it, it will perish. At least that is my fear. ... Poor mission of America! It is three years today since it was planned. It was on the feast of St. Bartholomew that I pronounced that 'yes' which bound me to the solitude of Indiana."

She spoke, too, of Bishop de la Hailandière, "who has one of those temperaments which makes martyrs of their possessors and still more of those who must put up with them from time to time. ... He is so pious, so humble, so zealous in the cause of religion, and especially for our house, that I consider it a duty for us to cast a veil over those faults which make him groan before God, and which do not touch essentials. ... He is jealous of his authority and wishes to do everything himself. ... It is not surprising that he wishes to do everything himself. Here superiors have the title of 'mother' and nothing more. One does not see a woman in this country involved in the smallest business affairs, the religious any more than the others. They stare at me in Terre Haute and elsewhere when they see me doing business, paying, purchasing..."

And finally, Mother Theodore confided to Mother St. Charles some of the personal changes she was experiencing. "I assure you that it makes me terribly afraid to take on myself alone the responsibility for a beginning community. ... Pray much for me, my good mother, for I have great need of it. I am dry and arid ... always busy with others, always distracted. ... The only thing I find the least bit reassuring is that I feel myself to be in the disposition to refuse God no sacrifice that he asks of me, to sacrifice especially the need I have always had to love and to be loved, to have someone to whom I can open my heart and be understood ... I no longer am concerned about myself."

Fire!

After ministering in Indiana nearly two years, the Sisters of Providence Congregation was growing. While monetary resources were scant, the summer crop had yielded a bountiful harvest. Though still recovering from the difficulties created by Father Buteux and Sister Aloysia, the sisters were settling into the new school year, enjoying the final days of autumn and finishing preparations for the long cold winter ahead. They were hopeful, confident that their mission would survive, when on the peaceful afternoon of October 2, 1842 — Mother Theodore's forty-fourth birthday — a devastating fire destroyed their barn and harvest.

The following day, with the sharp odor of burnt wood adrift in the air, Mother Theodore sat at her writing table and wrote to Mother Mary: "I had to tell you that I had just learned that a conspiracy was afoot to destroy our house. They began by prejudicing against us the families who had children here last year; only one returned, and that was only because she had no abode. ... Friday evening a boy I had sent to Terre Haute returned to me with a note from the merchant who had our confidence and who had been furnishing us all that we need. He wrote, then, on Friday, that henceforth he would give us nothing without the money. All those to whom we owed seemed to have agreed to come almost at the same time to demand their money...

"Fortunately, we had wheat, perhaps one hundred fifty bushels, about the same amount of oats, hay and corn shocks for our animals this winter. All that was safe in our big barn with other provisions such as bacon, suet, beds. ... Yesterday, then, was a day of retreat for the whole community, feast of the Holy Angels, feast of the Holy Rosary, it was the hour of recreation, but nevertheless silence reigned in the house; there was conversation only in my room, where a novice was asking counsel; we were conversing quietly when we saw a postulant running toward us, crying out that word which always makes one tremble, 'Fire! Fire!' In fact, there was a fire in our barn, about half a gun shot from our house. Within two minutes we were all assembled, armed with vessels for carrying water; we arrived running at the farm; already the flames were piercing the roof; we saw that all was sacrificed. ... In less than two minutes these two buildings, with carts, plows, etc. formed an immense hearth whence a bright twisting flame rose in the air to a prodigious height…

"We had no water, for we have neither well nor cistern; we take the water indispensable to us from a little spring which flows naturally and which scarcely suffices for the needs of the house; our only resource was the good God. I left everybody at work and went for a moment before our Lord to ask him to protect this house which was confided to him and where he deigned to live; fortified and filled with confidence, I returned to the workers…

"Nearly all had some burns, but by a special Providence, no one was seriously injured. … Our wheat, our poor wheat, all beaten down, burned before our eyes, is still burning as I write this. … Men watched all night near the fire so as to be able to do all they could to save our house, which is still in danger if there is the least wind; but it is so still that even the leaves on the trees are not moving. The good God has preserved us, and at this moment (eleven o'clock in the morning) everything gives hope that the worst is over." Mother Theodore then told Mother Mary, "This sad event seems to be the result of a crime; it seems impossible that a fire could have been kindled otherwise."

When they learned of the fire, Mother Theodore's superiors and her friends in France and New York sent gifts of money and letters of encouragement. The bishop of Vincennes sent sugar and coffee and one hundred dollars. In December, Bishop Bouvier wrote to Mother Theodore: "The letter you addressed October 3 to your superior general has torn my heart. The good God must have great designs on you since he tries you in this manner. … We continue to look upon you as daughters who are very dear to us; what you suffer touches us as though we were suffering ourselves. If Monsignor of Vincennes or other good souls do not look after you, how will you repair the effects of the disaster of which you are the victims? How are you going to provide food and keep? It is indeed a case of throwing yourselves with complete abandon into the hands of Providence."

5

Years of Growth and Years of Change

*If ever this poor little community becomes settled,
it will be established on the Cross; and that is
what gives me confidence and makes me hope,
sometimes even against hope.*

Mother Theodore Guerin

Merciless sharp winds from the north and the west battered the motherhouse at Saint Mary-of-the-Woods. Snow began falling early in November of 1842 and covered the ground throughout the winter, a frozen blanket of white. The barren, black forest was desolate.

Huddled in the convent, the Sisters of Providence struggled to conserve fuel, food and warmth and to care for the handful of pupils enrolled in the boarding school. From day to day, Mother Theodore did not know how she would feed the sisters and students entrusted to her care. She dismissed two of the farm hands because she could not pay them; she traded a little mill and some of the animals for wheat and corn. Still, she remained firm in her belief that God would provide.

In December, Mother Theodore noted in her journal: "It is a year since our good Mother has written to me or to any of us." Nevertheless, she wrote to Mother Mary in an attempt to tell her of the dire circumstances that resulted from the fire. "Since October 2, the day of our fire, nothing unusual has happened, but that mishap has caused us such poverty that we have been without the first necessities, such as bread; we have been three days without any. But the good Mr. Byerley lent us one hundred dollars, and Monsignor also borrowed an equal amount which he gave us for flour and other foodstuffs. For meat we are killing our own animals; we have exchanged others for oats and corn...

"As for money, one hardly sees it in the United States; they are completely ruined. People owe us almost a thousand dollars which equals more than five thousand francs of our money, and it is impossible to collect a cent. On the other hand, those to whom we are in debt torment us furiously; they must have their money at all costs. I paid about a hundred dollars of the money given me by Monsignor and Mr. Byerley, but that was like a drop of oil in the fire, it succeeded only in arousing their thirst for money. This lack of money might well be the cause of failure in this country where I had thought our Congregation was called to do great good."

In the same letter, she revealed some of Bishop de la Hailandière's recent actions: "... What makes us suffer most is the mania of this good bishop for changing the sisters. Recently we had decided to send another sister with Sister Liguori; he did not approve it. While I was in Vincennes, after having conducted the sisters to St. Francisville, I wished to visit our sisters in Jasper, as they were all upset, and Sister St. Vincent was ill; he did not approve of that either. He wants the establishments to depend on the priest, who would furnish the sisters with whatever they need. ... I have the greatest aversion to this kind of administration; it seems to me it would keep our sisters in a species of slavery; they could not even write a letter without the priests' knowledge. Besides, it would require too frequent contacts between them, and here above all this must not be, for the Protestants are always prepared to criticize actions the most innocent in themselves...

"I have to struggle against all these difficulties, hold myself firm against all that I believe would change the spirit of our institute and our dear Rules, but my good mother, I confess that I do it badly, I show that haughtiness of mine, above all with the bishop. I answer him by a blunt 'No,' or a 'Never, so long as I am superior.' ... I feel myself so empty. Above all it would be necessary to know how to pray, and I no longer know where my soul is. ... Here there are crosses and vexations of every kind. I can tell you, however, that personal crosses concern me very little; my heart is no longer capable of feeling; one would say that what it had suffered had covered it as with a breast plate which renders it insensible to every stroke. No, not to all — your silence causes me pain."

To Bishop Bouvier, Mother Theodore wrote: "My Lord, truly we have much to suffer in our deep forest, surrounded by enemies, having no other support, no other consoler than God alone. I in particular have trials which are personal, were it only that of having charge, almost alone, of a Congregation already numerous, to whom I have not always bread to give; and often I do not know where to procure what is absolutely necessary for the morrow, not counting the many contradictions which happen daily, and the fear of being burned down by our enemies...

"Permit me to thank you for the charity you had in sending

money to us. It was like a gift from heaven and is a new proof of the tender watchfulness of that Divine Providence, of which we are in truth the children. We had but one dollar remaining of what Mr. Byerley had lent us, and we did not know where to get a cent for the wants of the house. Still, how could I mistrust Divine Providence? Now I get flour on credit in the firm hope of soon being able to pay; so, my good Father, we have bread, shoes, etc., thanks to your liberality."

The situation at Saint Mary-of-the-Woods was aggravated by the money crisis in the United States. A notation, in Mother Theodore's handwriting, in the community diary in April of 1843 simply states: "The Illinois bank has failed; all the money we have is in that bank."

Searching for help

In February 1843, Mother Theodore again wrote to Mother Mary, this time to tell her that Bishop de la Hailandière had suggested that she travel to France to appeal for money for the Congregation. She wrote: "Monsignor told me two weeks ago that it will be impossible for him to provide for the expenses of our houses the coming year, let alone pay our debts. He told me then that he was thinking of sending me to France to appeal to our charitable friends on behalf of the foundation which promises so much and which he is unable to maintain. ... I have resolved to say nothing for or against, not wishing to take on myself the responsibility. But I would look upon it as a tender act of Providence if it were given to see you once again. ... It is to you that it belongs to found this house, to you, I say, who have grown old in the countless difficulties you have faced in doing God's work. ... It is almost impossible to say everything in letters at such a distance. It is difficult to be understood, when there is question of people so different in their customs. With what confidence, with what love I would receive your words, my good Mother! I think one learns to appreciate a mother more and more when one is so far from her."

In the midst of the turmoil and hardships engulfing the Congregation, Mother Theodore maintained her tender care of the Sisters of Providence at Saint Mary-of-the-Woods and the establishments. To the sisters teaching in Jasper, she offered a message of comfort and love. She did not mention the desperate situation at the motherhouse. Instead, she said, "Your letters have gladdened my heart and called forth more than one **Te Deum**, not for your victories, for you are not yet triumphant over your enemies, but for the sentiments you express. ... You may have to wait longer than you would like, you may have to bear privations; but, bear and forbear. Have confidence in the Providence that so far has never failed us. The way is not yet clear. Grope along slowly. Do not press matters; be patient, be trustful.

"I fully enter into all your difficulties; this is the same as telling you that I suffer with you. Need I tell you that I pray for you? Every thought of my dear sisters in Jasper is a prayer. You are lonesome, and so are we; but of this separation we do not complain. We cannot do our work if we all stay in the nest. At soon as the birds fly, they must be on the wing, looking after the interests of our Saviour Jesus. ... And rest assured, my dear daughters, if you lean with all your weight upon Providence, you will find yourselves well supported. ... Pray, be humble, be charitable, and God's blessing will be with you."

In March, Bishop de la Hailandière told Mother Theodore that he was leaving the decision about the voyage to France to her. "I will not oppose anything you may decide," he wrote in a brief note dated March 22, 1842. The bishop included a list of reasons for and against the voyage. "The object of this voyage must be to interest the faithful in your establishment," he wrote. "They can aid you by their prayers. ... They may procure novices for you. ... They can give you money. ..." The bishop hoped, too, that Mother Theodore could put to rest the false reports given to Mother Mary. His concerns centered on Mother Theodore's health, the morale of the sisters at Saint Mary-of-the-Woods during her absence, the possible failure of the journey, the expense, and the "probable effort of the motherhouse to counsel, regulate, direct everything here, directly or indirectly, to which I can no longer consent."

The Sisters of Providence Council met in April to discuss the wisdom of sending Mother Theodore to France to collect money and to meet with the Congregation's superiors. The sisters agreed that the journey was necessary, but they left the final decision to the bishop. According to a written account of that meeting, "After having weighed before God the reasons for and against, it was decided that these reasons be submitted to His Lordship Monsignor, the bishop of Vincennes, and that we would await his decision. ..." Bishop de la Hailandière quickly approved the voyage.

When Mother Theodore wrote to Mother Mary to tell her of the pending voyage, she did so with feelings of apprehension. Indeed, Mother Mary had not asked her to return to France. "We all think that this voyage is necessary for our beginning Congregation," she wrote. "I fear that you may consider it presumptuous to undertake it; but, my good mother, do not condemn us without hearing us. ... My heart is heavy; I am going to leave in the forest these poor children, these poor sisters who as I write this are far from suspecting what is threatening them, for I am in Vincennes where I have come with Sister Basilide to visit our establishments in Jasper and St. Francisville. ... On our arrival we learned that monsignor had taken all the precautions, all the arrangements for this voyage; it appears that he is going to send me alone, for he has no money; I still hope however that he will give me a companion, for I can find what is required for her passage in New York. ... Everyone says that I will not reach France. I do not know; I am not strong, the winter we have just passed has enfeebled me. But if it is the good God who has directed everything for this voyage, I have the confidence that he will sustain my feeble life as well on the waves as on the bed of sickness ... In all and everywhere may the will of God be done."

In the end, the bishop relented; Mother Theodore, accompanied by Sister Mary Cecilia, left Saint Mary-of-the-Woods on April 26. When they arrived at the home of Mrs. Parmentier in New York, a letter from Bishop de la Hailandière was awaiting Mother Theodore. "I approve this voyage," he wrote. "... Make known to the faithful your position and your needs; tell them that whatever I have done to establish you, much is lacking; that my resources are exhausted and that you have large debts." Included with the letter was a list of instructions. The bishop told Mother Theodore to seek prayers, novices (especially those skilled in music) and money. He included letters to Bishop Bouvier and Mother Mary, assuring them that he approved of the journey.

The thirty-day voyage aboard the ship **Silvia** was uneventful. Upon arriving in France, Mother Theodore and Sister Mary Cecilia were welcomed by the Sisters of Providence at Ruillé. Within a short time, however, it became evident that it was not a good time to solicit funds in France. Most of the people Bishop de la Hailandière told Mother Theodore to contact were away from the cities. Heavy rains had destroyed the crops in some regions of the country, and, in others, new laws had forced weavers to close their cottage industries. Money was scarce.

Eleven questions

In September, Mother Theodore met with Mother Mary, the Sisters of Providence Council and Bishop Bouvier. During the meeting, Mother Theodore presented a list of eleven questions. In a document dated September 12, 1843, Mother Theodore recorded the questions — and the answers she received.

- **First question:** What are the relations of the Congregation of Saint Mary-of-the-Woods with that of Ruillé? Answer: The Congregation of Saint Mary-of-the-Woods is a foundation from that of Ruillé. It must be self governing however under the authority of the bishop of Vincennes, its superior.

- **Second:** What help has the Congregation of Saint Mary-of-the-Woods a right to expect from that of Ruillé? Answer: None, except that of benevolence and charity.

- **Third:** Have the six sisters sent by the congregation of Ruillé the right to return to France if they wish? Answer: Yes, and they will always keep that right, since they went only on that condition.

- **Fourth:** Have the superiors of the congregation of Ruillé a right to give orders to the six sisters whom they have in America and to recall them? Answer: No, not without the consent of the bishop of Vincennes.

- **Fifth:** Does the congregation of Ruillé engage itself to pay the traveling expenses of any of its sisters who no longer wish to remain in America? Answer: The sisters should write to the superiors and await their response.

- **Sixth:** Have the sisters been given to the bishop of Vincennes to found a Congregation on the model of that of Ruillé in all that is possible or to found a Congregation according to the views of this prelate? Answer: The sisters have been given to His Lordship according to his request to form a Congregation on the model of that of Ruillé in all that is possible; and the desire of the bishop of Le Mans, of the superiors of Ruillé and especially of the Sisters of Saint Mary-of-the-Woods is that the Constitution and Rules be the same for the two congregations in all that is not absolutely impossible.

- **Seventh:** Should the changes which may be deemed necessary be made by the bishop of Vincennes without participation of the Council of Saint Mary-of-the-Woods? Answer: No, never, but if the bishop gives an order the sisters should obey and discuss the point when they find the opportunity.

- **Eighth:** May the bishop accept establishments and decide upon the conditions without consulting the Council? Answer: No, these things should be done together.

- **Ninth:** May the bishop admit to vesture or profession a postulant or novice who has not been presented to the Council? Answer: No, the Council must always regulate these things, but His Lordship has the right to refuse his approbation to a subject whom he judges undesirable even though she might have the votes of the Council.

- **Tenth:** May the bishop place and displace the sisters in the different employments of the Congregation? Answer: That is impossible.

- **Eleventh:** If the bishop does not approve that the superior or her delegates visit the establishments but if he does not forbid it, what should be done? Answer: She should visit her establishments. That is indispensable."

For Mother Theodore, the results of the meeting were bittersweet. While the meeting confirmed her actions with the bishop of Vincennes, the last thing she wanted to hear was that her Congregation was separate from the one in Ruillé.

In many regards, however, the outcome of the meeting regarding the separation was preordained. In June, Mother Mary wrote to Bishop Bouvier to question the motives behind Mother Theodore's visit. Mother Mary wrote, "Sister Theodore would seem to desire the union of the two congregations. This union does not seem possible in reality, for the superior general of Ruillé cannot be charged with the responsibility of a Congregation two thousand leagues from her residence; she cannot supervise the sisters, take part in the admission of subjects, nor in their dismissal, nor in the acceptance of establishments or their refusal, etc. It would be necessary to depend on what was written to her, exact or inexact, true or false…"

After the meeting in September, Mother Mary wrote to Sister Basilide: "Sister Theodore being in Paris, I am writing to you for the tranquility of your conscience and the peace of your soul. It seems to me that you have not rightly understood the purpose of your mission to America and the conditions under which you were given to your venerable prelate, and this misunderstanding causes painful difficulties in your dealings with your father and chief pastor, and you give each other pain because of this lack of understanding things which however seem to explain themselves.

"Six sisters from Ruillé were given to Monsignor the Bishop of Vincennes to form a Congregation of teaching sisters in his diocese on the model of that of Ruillé. The six sisters sent from Ruillé belong and will always belong to their congregation; they remain free to return to it, with, however, the consent of the bishop of Vincennes, but the superiors of the congregation of Ruillé cannot recall them. … The superiors of Ruillé do not pretend to exercise or to preserve rights over the new Congregation. So, my daughter, by considering well the authority of the Monsignor of Le Mans over our congregation, you will find the measure of the authority of the bishop of

Vincennes over yours. Try to conform to it. ... You will perhaps be pained to know the congregation of Ruillé is entirely separated from that of Vincennes. ... I beg you, my daughter, not to put the axe to the root for so small a thing; have patience and resignation, all will turn out for the best."

When the meeting at Ruillé was finished, Mother Theodore resumed her quest for aid. In Paris, she sought counsel with Bishop Bouvier: should she remain in France for the winter, or should she return to Saint Mary-of-the-Woods? She had collected barely enough money to pay for passage back to the United States. The bishop advised her to return to Indiana and assured her that he would contact the Congregation for the Propagation of the Faith about providing assistance to the mission at Saint Mary-of-the-Woods.

An audience with the queen

Before Mother Theodore left France, however, a chain of events instigated by friends of the Sisters of Providence of Saint Mary-of-the-Woods resulted in an audience with Queen Marié-Amélie, wife of King Louis Philippe. "At the hour stated, we went to the Tuilleries. We were ushered into the queen's apartment. She entered a moment later, gave us seats herself, and had us sit beside her, giving us the most gracious reception. She inquired about our situation like a tender mother and listened to the details with the greatest interest. She had the kindness to show particular benevolence toward Sister Mary Cecilia and spoke English with her," Mother Theodore wrote.

"Finally, after having manifested the most tender sympathy for our work, she asked us what we wished of her. We replied that as a single favor, we begged of her to pay our passage. She immediately answered: 'Your passage shall be paid. How many are you?' 'Four,' we answered; which was indeed true, since we had two postulants. 'Well,' she said, 'the voyage shall be paid for four.' Then she added, 'but this is not enough; you will need something when you are in your woods. I shall solicit here for you, and the king and my children will contribute. I shall ask them for you. But, on your side, you must do something also — you must ask the bishops to contribute; the bishop of Le Mans will no doubt do so.' "

Mother Theodore continued: "Thanks to the favor of the queen, we soon had that of several other persons. ... A number of persons of every station have shown such interest, such a desire for the prosperity of our work, and so many prayers have been and are still being offered, I doubt not but God will bless this dear little Congregation..."

While Mother Theodore was in Paris, she received a letter from Mother Mary, who had received letters from the sisters at Saint Mary-of-the-Woods.

Mother Mary wrote: "The most interesting news they give you is that Sisters Marie and Agnes pronounced their vows at the retreat which took place in the month of August and that, at the end of this retreat, the election of the superior general took place; you obtained five out of six votes, and consequently, you are still the superior of Saint Mary-of-the-Woods. ... The separation of the two congregations has also caused some pangs to poor Sister St. Francis. I have written to Sister Basilide that no opposition must be raised on this point; things are thus and could not possibly be otherwise. Finally, I continue to believe and to think that your presence is absolutely necessary to Saint Mary-of-the-Woods and that all the gold of France could not repair the harm that your absence can cause to the spiritual welfare of your beginning Congregation. ... Make haste, my dear Theodore, fly to Vincennes to mend the broken vessels, to watch over your flock. ... If your voyage to France has been useful, your presence at home is still more necessary."

Anticipating, perhaps, Bishop de la Hailandière's actions during Mother Theodore's absence and his reaction to the separation of the two congregations, Bishop Bouvier offered a bit of advice to him in a letter dated November 8, 1843. To Bishop de la Hailandière, Bishop Bouvier wrote: "Sister Theodore has been perfectly loyal to you. ... What she has obtained through your recommendations and mine together was given directly and only for her establishment. No other use could be made of it. Hence, I feel assured that, with the aid thus obtained and with what the Propagation already granted you for them, these devoted sisters will extricate themselves little by little. ... While Sister Theodore was traveling about with admirable devotedness on her begging mission, several letters arrived addressed to her. The superior thus learned that you had believed you might decide as to the admission of subjects, of their vocation, of their profession, etc., without considering the Constitutions and the Rule. She entreated me to make an observation to you that a Congregation could not be led in this manner. The bishop must have the superintendence and the high direction; but he must leave to the body its free action and abstain from whatever could appear arbitrary. ... Not only must he not force, he must not even urge the admission of anyone whomsoever, nor regulate their temporal affairs himself in any way whatsoever. The sisters have the management, as I said before, under his superintendence because he is their guardian and protector, but he does not manage for them. ... I cannot understand how you have, my lord, deposed Sister Theodore and caused an election during an absence endured in her quality of superior, and with your full consent given in writing."

Turmoil in Indiana

From the time Bishop de la Hailandière first mentioned the possibility of the trip to France, Mother Theodore feared what might occur if she left Saint Mary-of-the-Woods. She tried to anticipate any actions the bishop might take that would disrupt the sisters' lives.

While preparing for the journey, Mother Theodore and the sisters agreed to delay the annual retreat until after Mother Theodore returned from France. Mother Theodore gave Sister St. Francis Xavier the responsibility of looking after the community during her absence.

However, during the eleven months Mother Theodore was away from Saint Mary-of-the-Woods, Bishop de la Hailandière ruled the Congregation. He admitted novices to vows; closed the school at St. Francisville when he learned that village would be incorporated into the new Diocese of Chicago and moved the sisters who were teaching there; opened a new establishment; gave the habit of the Sisters of Providence to two women formerly of another congregation; directed the annual retreat; and called for the election of the superior. In all of these actions, he did not consult the sisters or refer to the Rule. During the election called by the bishop, Mother Theodore was elected superior, but Bishop de la Hailandière placed Sister Basilide in charge of the Congregation during her absence. Sister Basilide showed Mother Mary's letter about the separation of the Congregation to the bishop, and he, in turn, used the letter to justify his actions.

Journey home

Mother Theodore and her companions boarded the *Nashville* at Havre on November 28, 1843. Because winter was at hand, the ship sailed a southern route through the Gulf of Mexico. When the ship was about to enter the Mississippi River near New Orleans, Mother Theodore wrote to Mother Mary: "The dangers of the sea are past, and for us those dangers were great;

we have had a very bad crossing. Of the eight weeks we were on the ocean, we had forty days of very bad weather, almost constant tempests, but one was frightful; the sailors said they had never in their lives witnessed the like. ... If the Lord had not come to our assistance, it would have been the end of us. ... We prayed a great deal. We made vows ... but especially we invoked Mary and St. Anne, her august mother; it is to them that we owe our safety." It was during this furious storm that Mother Theodore promised to honor St. Anne with a novena.

Mother Theodore did not finish the letter to Mother Mary until February 6, 1844, when she wrote from New Orleans: "My good mother, I am finishing this letter at the convent of the Ursulines, where I have been ill for ten days. It seems that this illness will be of long duration, for my strength is exhausted, and I can take very little nourishment. ... I am obliged to separate myself from my dear Sister Mary Cecilia; she will leave with our other companions for Saint Mary-of-the-Woods, and I must stay here. I always find new sacrifices to make when I think it is the end."

In January, though still very ill, Mother Theodore wrote to Bishop Bouvier: "There was a letter awaiting me here from the sisters at Saint Mary-of-the-Woods. Since the last news I received at Ruillé, His Lordship has formed two new establishments, withdrawn the sisters from one which we had, given the habit to two postulants, admitted two novices to their vows, and received three sisters from another community — all without the advice or consent of the sisters. ... Ask for me the spirit of understanding and of counsel. I shall need both gifts if the Lord sends me to Vincennnes..."

Later in the spring, Mother Theodore wrote to M. Léon Aubineau, an editor of the *Univers* in France. In her journal account, which was published in the *Univers*, she painted vivid images of the voyage and spoke of her ministries among the passengers. She wrote: "In the steerage there was the worst kind of rabble you can imagine. Quarreling, drunkenness, fighting, blaspheming — every kind of vice was to be met with there. It was in truth a very antechamber of hell. I do not know why it was that they treated us with respect; yet, if any of them was ill, the others would stand by in two rows for me to pass through whenever I went to attend them. They chose me to baptize a newly born infant. I felt a deep sense of gratitude for this favor…"

She shared with the editor some of the sights she saw in New Orleans, including one which touched her deeply: "The most painful sight I saw in New Orleans was the selling of slaves. Every day in the streets of appointed places, negroes and negresses in holiday attire are exposed for this shameful traffic. This spectacle oppressed my heart. … I would have wished to buy them all that I might say to them, 'Go! Bless Providence. You are free!' "

Mother Theodore also revealed her feelings upon arriving again in Indiana: " … With inexpressible joy I saw once more my Indiana. I would have loved to kiss its soil. This land was no longer for me the land of exile; it was the portion of my inheritance, and in it I hope to dwell all the days of my life."

6

Years of Sorrow

Love all in God and for God, and all will be well.
Mother Theodore Guerin

As Mother Theodore returned to Indiana, she knew beyond a doubt that she shared the responsibility for the Sisters of Providence at Saint Mary-of-the-Woods with God's Providence alone. Acknowledging the immense challenge of nurturing and administrating the new Congregation, Mother Theodore prayed for God's blessing and guidance, squared her shoulders and accepted the responsibility. She knew that all things were possible with God and for God.

Mother Theodore's concerns were many, but she did not know she was entering into years of heart-wrenching sorrow and soul-wearying trials that would place the very existence of the Congregation in jeopardy. Throughout these long, sad years, Mother Theodore continued to seek solace and counsel from her dear friend, Bishop Bouvier. She was comforted and strengthened, too, by new friends in the United States, including Father John Corbe, who was named chaplain of the Sisters of Providence Congregation in 1842.

The sorrows and trials stemmed from increased interference by Bishop de la Hailandière. The bishop was a troubled man, but he was not evil. He did not have experience — and the subsequent skills — in managing a diocese, especially one as rugged as Vincennes, nor of working with women religious. Regardless of his actions, which frequently were contradictory and unreasonable, Mother Theodore always considered that he acted out of zeal and with the best of intentions. Mother Theodore respected Bishop de la Hailandière. She obeyed his wishes until he began interfering with the internal governance of the Congregation and demanding procedures that opposed the Sisters of Providence Rule. Bishop de la Hailandière's belief that — as a bishop — he possessed total control over the Sisters of Providence was not unique. Historians note that other bishops who were educated in France and later settled in the United States held similar notions. Some refused to relinquish control even when limits to their power were established by the Sacred Congregation of Bishops and Regulars in Rome. Ultimately, Mother Theodore had no choice but to stand up to Bishop de la Hailandière. To have done otherwise would have been unfaithful to the Rule and to her duty as superior general of the Congregation. Even then, and even when she trembled as she awaited his orders, Mother Theodore treated the bishop with compassion.

Aware as she was of some of the events that transpired while she was in France, Mother Theodore approached Vincennes and a meeting with the bishop with more than a little trepidation. She visited first the house of the four Sisters of Providence the bishop had assigned to teach at Vincennes. There, after sharing a simple meal, Mother Theodore and Sister St. Vincent sat alone for a time. Sister St. Vincent said the bishop had declared that he would not allow Mother Theodore to return to Saint Mary-of-the-Woods. In her journal and in letters to Bishop Bouvier, she recorded the meeting with the bishop. "The next day, after hearing Mass and seeking in Holy Communion the strength needed, grieved but calm and submissive, and accompanied by Sister St. Vincent, I went to see the bishop. ... He began to reproach me with the gravest and bitterest reproaches about things which I heard in astonishment; for not only did he relate to me under the blackest colors all that I had in the past said and proposed to the Council, but also a number of other things that I had never even thought of. ... His Lordship then changed the conversation to speak about the money he said I had stolen from him in Paris. He said I would have to refund it to him and immediately, too...

"Our interview lasted two hours. I was exhausted. I trembled, fearing to hear the fatal order to retire forever without being allowed to see again those poor children at Saint Mary's, who were so impatiently awaiting me. ... I asked for and obtained permission to retire, but His Lordship directed me to return the next day. He said he was not through with me yet. ... The following day we returned and found Monsignor a little less ill disposed through one of the providential and loving dispositions of our God. ... Believing the moment favorable, I asked permission to write a few words to the sisters to announce my arrival. It was granted, and upon the bishop's desk itself, I wrote a note saying I would leave for Saint Mary's by the first steamboat. ... Among the countless accusations heaped upon me, one was that I was not sick at all at New Orleans, but had remained there to plot something against my superior. The state of weakness, however, to which I was reduced was my justification. ... The next day I was at Saint Mary's."

There, with the sisters, Mother Theodore went first to the chapel to kneel in thanksgiving before the Blessed Sacrament. Rejoicing to be together once again, Mother Theodore and the sisters resumed their work. The spring of 1844 was a busy one. With the gifts she received in France, Mother Theodore began paying off the debts that had accumulated after the fire. The dire poverty of the past several months was finished. Though the sisters' lifestyle remained frugal, there was sufficient food in the pantry.

With the coming of warm, sunshine-washed days, work began in the gardens and fields. The Congregation purchased another cow for milk and four calves. Ever mindful of the young girls boarding at the Academy, Mother Theodore developed plans to preserve the summer's bounty of fresh fruit so it could be served to pupils during the cold and dreary winter months ahead. It was during this time, too, that the Congregation established, in keeping with the Rule, a pharmacy where they dispensed remedies to their neighbors in the surrounding countryside. And, finally, Mother Theodore oversaw the construction of a small cabin, built of logs, that would serve for years to come as a shrine to St. Anne.

It was also during this time that Mother Theodore became better acquainted with Father Corbe. Truly, as the months flowed into years, Mother Theodore and the Sisters of Providence considered Father Corbe's presence at Saint Mary-of-the-Woods to be a gift from Providence. The "good Father Corbe," as they referred to him, was gentle, intelligent and devoted. A long-time friend of Bishop de la Hailandière, Father Corbe sometimes was able to soften the bishop's harsh judgments, words and deeds. In the end, Father Corbe contributed greatly to the survival of the Congregation.

As life at the motherhouse returned to normal, Mother Theodore began planning visits to the establishments. She had not visited the sisters at Jasper for more than two years, and she had never seen the mission at St. Peter's, which the bishop opened while she was in France. Knowing the bishop did not endorse visits to the establishments, but determined as ever to obey the Rule, Mother Theodore stopped first at Vincennes to speak with him.

Mother Theodore and Bishop de la Hailandière had clarified some of their misunderstandings, so the meeting was cordial. In a letter to Bishop Bouvier, she wrote, "… I went to see His Lordship. He could not have been more friendly. He wished again to make excuses to me. I assured him that that was not necessary, that very candidly I had forgotten the past, that it was even impossible for me to think of anything personal when I saw the existence of our poor little house so seriously compromised. I added that we would ask but one thing, to be able to observe our Rule in his diocese…"

The mission at St. Peter's

Counted among Mother Theodore's concerns during this time were the living conditions of the sisters who were teaching away from Saint Mary-of-the-Woods. Poverty, poor diets and exposure to the sweltering humidity in summer and the frigid cold in winter left the sisters exhausted and susceptible to illness. Tuberculosis was prevalent. These factors, combined with the physical and spiritual hardships inherent in life on the frontier, frequently led to early death.

When Bishop de la Hailandière opened the mission at St. Peter's, the two sisters he assigned there were given the use of two long-vacant log cabins. In April 1844, Sister St. Liguori, wrote to Mother Theodore: "… This winter, as we had so little wood, we stayed in the kitchen after school hours. If the winter had been a severe one, I think we would have frozen as the wind, the rain and snow came in from above and below and on the sides. … Last Saturday night our table was covered with snow. … The poor establishment of St. Peter's has had a melancholy beginning. ... On our leaving Vincennes, the bishop gave us a clock, a few school books and nineteen dollars. With this sum, small considering our needs, we have added very little to our furnishings. The Congregation has raised a subscription of thirty-some dollars to assist us, most of it paid in corn, wheat, flour, soap, etc., which have been of great utility to us. ... We have milk in abundance. This enables us to economize on coffee, tea and even meat, for a bowl of milk and a piece of bread make a delicious meal..."

Devoted as they were to their work, the sisters at St. Peter's were happy, but when Mother Theodore visited the mission in May, she wept when she saw the way the sisters lived. She wrote to Bishop Bouvier: "On arriving at St. Peter's, we found both of the sisters sick. They were prostrate with fatigue and want. ... Their log house is open to every wind, and inside there is nothing, nothing! ... not a key to lock out not only the thieves but even the wild animals that would enter their cabin. Every night we were obliged to draw up a school desk against the door to keep it closed."

Mother Theodore left St. Peter's determined to compile strict guidelines to be followed when establishments were opened in the future. Among the requirements she presented to the bishop for approval a few weeks later were that the sisters would receive the income from the schools and would give an accounting of it only to their superior; that, in keeping with the Sisters of Providence Rule, provisions would be made for a free school; and that a furnished house would be provided for the sisters. The bishop looked at the guidelines and said, "Do as you wish; do whatever seems best. I approve in advance of all that you will do."

Sorrows

In June, Mother Theodore wrote to Bishop Bouvier to tell him of a visit with Bishop de la Hailandière, who, only a few weeks earlier had apologized for his behavior. "I asked only one thing, to be able to follow our Rule in his diocese," she wrote. "He answered graciously that our rules were very wise, that he wished them to be followed, and he added, 'You can observe them all here as in France, with the exception of the foundation of establishments. I desire nothing more than to see them observed. ... I am going to give you the land which remains; I have sold a part, but ... I will not give any more money, and you must return mine.' ... I left enchanted and conversing interiorly with you and with our Mothers; I flattered myself that I would be able to please you by writing all that, telling you that we could follow all our Rules, that the land was ours; it is true that we would receive nothing more from Monsignor, but no matter, poverty did not frighten us..."

In the same lengthy letter, Mother Theodore told Bishop Bouvier about the next message she received from Bishop de la Hailandière. In that letter, the bishop declared, "Less than ever I have the desire to involve myself in your affairs." Mother Theodore wrote, "... This letter greatly surprised me; I was not less surprised when I learned that His Lordship wrote another letter to our chaplain in which he told him to sell the bricks which are in our yard and which had been made in the spring to add wings to our boarding school which is falling and which has become too small..."

Finally, Mother Theodore asked Bishop Bouvier, "What do you wish us to do? Remain here? In that case we must resign ourselves to not being able to fulfil our Rules and to form a house which, directed as Monsignor wishes, would perhaps do more harm than good. Should we return to France? But in that case, what shall we do with these poor girls who have left all that was dear to them in the world to come and ask us to lead them to God? What is to be done with the money which charity has given us for the good of the mission? These, Monsignor, are questions that I put to you with a heart full of grief, for having received this dear mission of Vincennes from your hands, you know whether I love it. … If your paternal goodness can find us the means of saving ourselves while working for the salvation of others, use it. … I beg you not to abandon us, we have only you for refuge. Have pity on your poor daughters of the woods."

In August, the Congregation agreed to establish a school at Madison, a small town along the Ohio River in southern Indiana. True to her resolve to watch out for the safety and well being of the sisters on mission, the agreement included a house for two sisters and a hundred-dollar payment to each sister the first year. The priest in Madison, Father Julian Delaune, also said he would pay the sisters' expenses when they returned to Saint Mary-of-the-Woods in the summer for retreat.

The fragile calm that existed between Bishop de la Hailandière and the Congregation was shattered when he ordered the school in Vincennes to accept, as boarders, two students originally destined for Saint Mary-of-the-Woods. The school in Vincennes, at the time, was not boarding students. As administrator of the Congregation, it was Mother Theodore's duty to make decisions regarding the schools. When she pointed out that the bishop's action was in conflict with the Rule, he was enraged. In July, he relinquished his role as ecclesiastical superior of the Sisters of Providence Congregation and gave the title and the responsibility to Father Corbe.

Writing to Father Corbe, Bishop de la Hailandière said he did not understand why Father Corbe sent Mother Theodore to speak with him. The bishop said he asked Mother Theodore, "But in what do I oppose your following your Rule, I who never interfere in your affairs? What have I regulated or commanded contrary to your Constitutions? I oppose your Rules! Rest assured, that will be so no longer. For I have asked Father Corbe to be my delegate. … He will be your local superior."

In October of 1844, the bishop again wrote to Father Corbe, "… As bishop of Vincennes, and whatever they may say to the contrary, I positively forbid that any sister be sent or remain all alone in an establishment, that anyone travel alone without a special permission from you or from me. Let none of them go out of the diocese. As for the mother, I am opposed to her visiting her establishments without a written permission from the bishop, or in my absence from the diocese, from you alone. …" The bishop feared, and with just cause, that Mother Theodore might move the Sisters of Providence to another diocese.

As December of 1844 drew near, Mother Theodore recorded the events of the past several weeks in a letter to Bishop Bouvier. "Our boarding school being too small for the number of pupils who present themselves, and His Lordship having expressed the desire that we build at our own expense, we felt we should propose it to our sisters, but all unanimously refused to give their approval to this enterprise. In fact, it involved building on land that did not belong to us; contracting for that purpose a debt of more than twenty thousand francs; building on a land where it would be necessary to use and pay for the owner's bricks, follow his plan which is fine but expensive, and with all that not have the freedom to put, at this moment, a little bannister on a stairway on which our children are in danger every day of killing themselves; to replace by a few planks the brick pavement of a damp room which serves as classroom during the day and dormitory at night; not to go through such or such a place because it would disturb this or that which will have to be done later; and finally to cover all the expense, to contract debts on the uncertain resources of a boarding school which was composed yesterday of twenty-seven pupils, today of twenty-five, and tomorrow … I don't know. …

"Knowing that Monsignor was to come to bless the church of the village, I believed I should prepare to see him by prayer and retreat; I was persuaded, as we all were, that this visit would decide our future. … I had lined up what I proposed to say to Monsignor; it resolved itself into three things which I felt would force us to leave the diocese: first, the impossibility of establishing our Congregation, being on bad terms with Monsignor, this misunderstanding having been made public by the bishop himself. Second: that being only the stewards of the community we could not in conscience build on land that did not belong to it. Third, and most important: that we could not remain in a place where we were not permitted to follow the sacred obligations which we had contracted with God by our profession…

"He told me that the community was his and that it would always remain his, that if I were not content I could leave alone and at once if I wished; he added emphatically as he pointed out to me our little cabin: 'I am the proprietor, spiritual and temporal, of that house; I am going to forbid you to set foot in it.' The good God gave me the grace to remain calm. Little by little Monsignor calmed down. … He left us without deciding anything, telling us that soon he would leave for France. In fact, five days after his arrival in Vincennes, Father Martin wrote us that Monsignor had left and had appointed him his vicar general…

"We ask two things of Monsignor the bishop of Vincennes: that he approve our Rules, and that he give us this land. On these conditions we will always remain in Indiana. … We beg you to give us the permission to go and establish ourselves in another diocese. It would be better not to have the Congregation at all than to have one that would have no other rule than the caprices of a disordered imagination, which will condemn tomorrow what it commands today."

Mother Theodore went on to tell Bishop Bouvier that she hoped reconciliation was possible. She pointed out that the Congregation had grown in public opinion: "Those who were our declared enemies now give us their children to raise. They take pride in protecting our institute. ... We have paid our debts, we pay cash for what we buy. This is enough to give us, in the eyes of these men of money, what they call 'respectability' ... In our five establishments we have about two hundred Catholic children who console us by their docility and their simplicity. They have made their First Communion with admirable sentiments everywhere, but especially at Madison. There the sisters are mocked; they throw stones on them in the streets, insult them, but already the most bigoted, the most relentless against them are becoming appeased; two of them even sent their daughters to them. The children lose their prejudices in our classes and then make their parents lose theirs. ... We have twenty-five boarders here. ... Our American sisters are doing very well. ... All love our Congregation sincerely and are prepared to make every kind of sacrifice to follow our Rules. ... Frankly, my Father, I do not know whether I could live without afflictions. They give me confidence; I am permitted to receive Holy Communion often, and that is where I find the strength to submit."

A measure of Mother Theodore's despair — and hope — is evident in a letter she wrote to Father Martin in January of 1845: "... If ever this poor little community becomes settled, it will be established on the Cross; and that is what gives me confidence and makes me hope, sometimes even against hope."

While Bishop de la Hailandière was in France, Bishop Bouvier spoke with him but to no avail. Finally, Bishop Bouvier advised Mother Theodore that if all attempts to work in harmony with Bishop de la Hailandière failed, the Congregation should leave the Diocese of Vincennes.

In the spring of 1845, Mother Theodore replied: "The permission that you and our good Mother gave us to try elsewhere has made us experience a real joy. ... But what would become of our dear American sisters? The mere idea of leaving them bruises our hearts. And then, what would become of our Catholic pupils who give us so much consolation? ... We will make one more attempt. If it does not succeed, we shall leave, but I have interiorly the confidence that the good God wishes us in America. If he wished to destroy us, would he send us so many crosses? That precious Cross which has always been the seal of his works? I cannot believe it."

While in Europe, Bishop de la Hailandière offered his resignation to Pope Gregory XVI, who rejected it. When he returned to Indiana in October of 1845, his dissatisfaction with Mother Theodore was at its peak.

In December, Mother Theodore wrote to Bishop Peter Paul Lefevre, the bishop of the Diocese of Detroit, about the possibility of relocating in that state. Many priests had left the Diocese of Vincennes because of their own conflicts and disagreements with Bishop de la Hailandière, and they, too, were seeking dioceses that would welcome the Sisters of Providence.

No one, perhaps, was more miserable than Bishop de la Hailandière. In a letter dated December 24, 1842, he wrote: "In the midst of so many difficulties, and being of so great an incapacity, I fear to lose my soul. That is why I beg his Eminence to examine before the good God whether it would not be expedient that I cease to occupy the See of Vincennes. ..." He repeated the offer to resign in January of 1845. In January of 1846, he wrote, "The mission confided to me has always seemed a charge much beyond my strength."

In March of 1846, Father Simon Lalumiere of Terre Haute wrote to the bishop of Baltimore: "It is three years since I wrote you about the misfortune of our poor diocese, all in consequence of our bishop. ... I only appeal to you as the father of the American church to see into the matter. ..." In May of 1847, Father Julien Benoit wrote to Father Martin: "The bishop has perceived that there is nothing for him to gain in trying to plague me, and he leaves me in peace. It is not the same for the poor Sisters of Providence."

In January of 1846, Mother Theodore issued a final plea to Bishop de la Hailandière. Weary, ill and sorrowing, she offered to retire as superior general of the Congregation. She wrote: "... I find that it is time to come to an end. One word only, it will be the last. ... I proposed to you many times that I abandon this dear Congregation that I love so much and for which I asked God to let me continue to live, not exacting, not asking anything of you except that you adopt, that you protect this Congregation, that you approve the Rules, or that you give others, so that the members which compose it know their obligations and their privileges. ... My conscience is my witness that I have done all that I could to avoid this misfortune, for I love Indiana with my whole soul. To do good there, to see our Congregation solidly established there before I die, was my whole ambition; the good God has permitted that you did not wish it; may his will be done."

In January of 1846, the Congregation incorporated its institute with the State of Indiana. In a Letter Circular distributed to the sisters in March 1846, Mother Theodore wrote, in part: "... the moment has come when we must leave the distressing state in which we have been for so long a time." The circular contained a letter, signed by members of the Congregation's Council and addressed to Bishop de la Hailandière. In the letter, the sisters reiterated their requests: "Your Lordship knows that we have never asked aught but these things in order to establish ourselves in Indiana as a Congregation subject to you. Many times you have said, and even written, that you intended to grant us these things, but that we had put obstacles. These obstacles are now all removed — all the Sisters of Providence can now hold property legally; therefore we dare hope that you will not delay to give us this last proof of your good will. ... However, faithful to the spirit of candor which we have always followed, we must say that, after all that has occurred since our first request, your silence, or any reply which would not be the acts we ask for, could not but be regarded by us, this time, as a formal refusal; in which case we would consider ourselves obliged to take a definitive resolution, and that with very little delay. ... The fate of our Congregation is yet in your hands. ..."

Bishop de la Hailandière, in turn, demanded an "Act of Reparation" from the sisters, because he believed they had spoken against him to their superiors in France. While the sisters had written and spoken only the truth about their dealings with the bishop, they agreed — in order to attain peace — to sign a retraction. In July, Mother Theodore issued another Letter Circular to the sisters: "... our affairs are at last terminated. Our bishop has granted what we asked — what we asked with so much importunity — the approbation of our holy Rules and the property of Saint Mary's. He has pardoned us everything that, in our days of difficulty, he thought wanting in respect. ... We in turn have promised in the name of the Congregation that we will remain in the Diocese of Vincennes; this, then is the portion of the vineyard of the Lord which we are called upon to cultivate..."

In a letter to Mother Mary, Mother Theodore said: "We resolved to sign it. ... Monsignor cannot make up his mind to pardon entirely women who have provoked him beyond endurance, and especially her who, he says, leads them like sheep."

That spring, after visiting the establishments, Mother Theodore stopped in Vincennes, where she met with the bishop. Her account of that meeting follows: "The next day His Lordship told me that I would do well to see him alone. I went. I spare you our interview … for it lasted four hours. The end and purpose of it was to make me consent to ask him in writing if I might return to France. … I did not weep; I believe that the source of my tears is dried up…"

The bishop's unpredictable behavior continued. In July, he presented a deed to the property at Saint Mary-of-the-Woods to the Congregation. Mother Theodore recorded the event in a letter to Bishop Bouvier: "He came the fourteenth of this month; he brought us the deed for part of the land at St. Mary's, about eighty or ninety acres; he is keeping the rest. The deed contains conditions which displease our sisters very much; for example, we will not be permitted to do the least thing on our land without the permission of His Lordship or his heirs, etc. As the laws of this country do not permit conditions, it is probable that the deed will not be valid; I took it to a lawyer who will examine it and tell us whether it is legal or not. I tremble lest it be badly drawn…"

She also announced that the Academy was being enlarged. "… It was not possible to wait longer before beginning to build. They have been working on our house for ten days. Monsignor donated his bricks with three thousand francs received for us from the Propagation of the Faith last year, but which he had not yet given to us. The whole will cost from twenty-five to thirty thousand francs. … We now have forty-six pupils in our boarding school; although they do not all pay, we have been able to set something aside this year. This boarding school is our only source of support for the priest's house, our novitiate, our establishments, five orphans and the boarding school itself. … Our establishments are doing much good. We have been greatly consoled in our visitations this year. We are opening a new house after retreat at Fort Wayne, in the northern part of the state; they propose to give us a brick house with a garden and a little meadow; this is all they can do; we shall have to get settled at our own expense, as elsewhere."

In October, Mother Theodore again wrote to Bishop Bouvier, this time to tell him about a secret election Bishop de la Hailandière attempted to conduct after the sisters' retreat. "Monsignor arrived with the retreat master and said nothing about the election until the eve of the general Communion. ... The sisters, informed of the Monsignor's intentions, consulted Father Corbe about what was best to do. It was decided that they represent to His Lordship that an election was impossible, since there was only one candidate who could be elected, according to the Rule ... Monsignor refused to listen to anything; he said it was a revolt against legitimate authority, that henceforth he would not set a foot in our house, not even for the next day's ceremonies. ... Monsignor kept his word with respect to his last threat. From the day of which I speak, he has treated us as strangers. ... He told us we were no longer a religious Congregation, that the power to govern had been taken away from us and that consequently there was no merit in obedience.

"Of all the crosses that it has pleased the good God to send me since I have been in America, this one weighs most heavily on my heart. By remaining here against the will of my bishop, I have obeyed, it is true, the superior he had given us. ... Am I not in a place so filled with stumbling blocks against the will of God? If so, am I not going to lose myself and attract a host of spiritual and temporal evils on this poor little Congregation? It seems to me that the good God will no longer bless us, and without his help, what will become of this work? I am a proud, imperious, haughty daughter who for more than twenty years has been commanding without ever having learned to obey. ..."

At the end of the letter, Mother Theodore added a hurried note: "I must finish in order to leave immediately for Madison where Sister Liguori is very ill. Another of our sisters is dying in Jasper."

Mother Theodore's quick departure to be with Sister Liguori left unfinished business at the motherhouse. During a stop in Edinburgh, Indiana, she wrote to the sisters at Saint Mary-of-the-Woods, giving them instructions on what they should do in her absence. "… All those who have not yet put on warm underclothing should do so without delay. The mornings and evenings are too cold; it is a good thing I was asked to bring the old cloak. I ask Sister Olympiade to see to it that our good and dear Father Corbe has all his winter garments in good condition, especially if he leaves for Vincennes; it is cold in the carriages. … I also ask my sisters at the boarding school to see that the children are warmly dressed. … I am writing to you with a piece of steel that they call a pen; I am obliged to plunge it into the bottom of a bottle to get some ink, at the peril of the whiteness of my fingers. … You see, at least, my well-beloved, that I have no need of searching very deep into my heart to find there the tender love with which it is filled for all of you." She added a postscript: "If Monsignor's shoes have come back from the shoemaker, you must send them to him; that will keep his feet warm."

Mother Theodore remained in Madison several weeks before returning to Saint Mary-of-the-Woods. In January 1847, she wrote to Mother St. Charles: "… Our forests are so frozen that it is impossible for us to go even to Terre Haute. It may be that our dear Sister Liguori is dead now; for twelve days we have been unable to receive news of her because of the bad weather. … It is twenty-two years today, my good mother, that I left you for the first time to go to an establishment. … Who would have said that day that there would come a time when you would let more than five years go by without giving a sign of remembrance to the one you then called your dear daughter! ... We think then that this time I shall receive orders to leave as soon as it is possible to travel; but perhaps I shall have left for the great voyage before that, for I feel already the stirrings of the cruel illness which each winter brings me to the brink of eternity. I have never fully recovered from my last attack; it carried off all my strength and my eyes. I can neither read nor write unless my nose is adorned with a pair of glasses which help me to distinguish black from white." The closing words of the letter reflect Mother Theodore's abiding faith in Providence, for she wrote: "From the hand of so good a Father, nothing but good can come."

In a letter dated January 29, 1847, Mother Theodore notified the sisters of the death of Sister Mary Liguori: "In feelings of grief, the most keen and profound, we come to announce to you the loss we have sustained in the death of our dearly beloved Sister Mary Liguori Tiercin. It pleased God to take her away from our tenderness this morning at eight o'clock after a cruel illness which she bore for three months and a half ..." Then, in the early morning hours of February 17, the Congregation suffered its second death, that of young Sister Seraphine Carroll.

The crisis

In the spring of 1847, as was her way, Mother Theodore, accompanied by Sister Mary Xavier, left the Sisters of Providence at Saint Mary-of-the-Woods to visit her establishments, now scattered from one end of Indiana to the other. She traveled first to Fort Wayne, and from there took the canal to Cincinnati, where she boarded a steamboat for the voyage down the Ohio River to Madison. Along the way, she wrote to Sister St. Francis Xavier. "... I shall not be long in Vincennes if I am permitted to leave when I wish."

A few days later, on May 17, Mother Theodore received a message and a warning from Father Corbe: "I urge you not to enter into any discussion with His Lordship. If he mentions elections, you will be able to save yourself by simply telling him that if the community wishes it, you will not object; if he tries to force you to resign, or asks you to sign or consent to some proposition, protect yourself by leaving the decision to the community. The good God, I hope, will aid you. Despite my confidence in God, my soul is sad. It is indeed weary of this kind of warfare. For so long a time no rest, no peace, and such a feeble hope for the future. ... Come now, my dear Mother Theodore, pray hard to the Blessed Virgin and she will bring you back to us. ..."

In Vincennes, Mother Theodore visited the school and stayed with the Sisters of Providence in their house. On the day before she was to leave for Saint Mary-of-the-Woods, after reserving a place in the stagecoach for the following morning, she went to see Bishop de la Hailandière. Sister St. Francis Xavier recorded the fateful events that followed: "I shall relate only the end of her conversation with His Lordship. He accused her of wishing to remain superior, despite everything. Mother then offered to propose an election to the assembled community, and if they accepted it, she would consider herself freed from the duties of her charge; but until such time she would not leave her daughters."

At the end of the interview, the bishop told Mother Theodore she must remain in his house until she agreed to all of his demands. She replied that she would never agree to everything. The bishop left the room, locked the door and went to dinner. Historians record the rest of that evening: "The sisters, not knowing where Mother Theodore was, went later in the day to the bishop to find out. He unlocked the door; Mother Theodore fell on her knees, begging his blessing. He blessed her and silently motioned her out." The sisters took Mother Theodore to their home, but later that evening, May 20, 1847, the bishop went to the sisters' house to announce his sentence against Mother Theodore.

According to Sister St. Francis Xavier: "The bishop declared to our Mother that not only was she no longer the superior but that she was not now even a Sister of Providence, for he released her from her vows; that she had to leave the diocese immediately and go elsewhere to hide her disgrace; that he forbade her to write to the sisters at Saint Mary's — they had no need of her letters."

Sister St. Francis Xavier also described the events that took place at Saint Mary-of-the-Woods: "... We were trembling here, and we were praying to God, when a letter dated from Vincennes arrived to reassure us. Our mother wrote from that city that she was going to leave the following day without having seen Monsignor, and that we could send the carriage to Terre Haute the following Saturday.

"The next morning about nine o'clock, we saw in the distance the blessed carriage headed toward Saint Mary's. 'Sisters, there is our Mother!' cried Sister Olympiade. 'Come to the chapel and thank the good God!' We thanked him with all our hearts and then ran quickly to meet Mother. The carriage was empty; Sister Marie was walking sadly toward the bridge. ... 'Where is Mother?' we all cried together. 'Where is Mother? Is she ill?' 'Oh, she could not come! Monsignor has driven her from the Congregation; he has forbidden her to return here,' said Sister Marie.

"...Our Father Corbe had promised Monsignor to propose an election to the community; he did so. 'You know my personal opinion,' he said to Sister Francis Xavier, 'however, it is necessary to know the dispositions of the community. Tell your sisters that, if they yield to Monsignor's views, he will love and protect them; that if they oppose his views, they run the risk of sharing their Mother's fate.'"

" 'No, no, no election!' all cried together. 'We will follow our Mother wherever she will go.'"

" 'You must know,' added Sister St. Francis Xavier, weeping, 'that Monsignor has said that he would excommunicate all the sisters who would leave his diocese without his permission. He will not let them take away the least thing and perhaps will have them followed by the police. On the contrary, those who remain will have the land of Saint Mary-of-the-Woods and the protection of their bishop together with his confidence.' There was not a single sister in the community who hesitated between her duty and the sad future which would be the consequence of it. 'We will no longer have anything,' they said. 'We will be considered by Monsignor as the reproach of the world, but we shall have done our duty.'"

"…We wrote together a letter which we sent to our Mother … Our workmen set down their tools and wept; then they took counsel, and their deliberation was like ours: they resolved to leave Saint Mary's. … It was resolved that our faithful gardener, Jean Delahaye, would go immediately to carry our resolution to our Mother, and to bring her back if it were possible.

"He traveled all night and arrived in Vincennes Sunday morning during Mass. He immediately delivered our letters to our Mother, who was very much consoled to see our courageous resolution and yet saddened by thinking of the results she could foresee. … We had placed in trunks the things we wished to take with us. But to whom should we address them? … We wrote to the archbishop of Baltimore about what had occurred; we also informed our superiors in France. … But we put our hope in God alone…

"On May 25, Jean came back from Vincennes, but he came back alone; our Mother was too ill to accompany him, and even if she had been well she would not have wished to return against the will of Monsignor. … Friday, when Father Corbe was in Terre Haute, he suddenly saw a man on horseback who asked for him; he recognized a Frenchman from Vincennes. 'Here is a letter from the Mother,' he said. 'She is very ill.' Our Father Corbe read in haste; he saw that our Mother was asking for him because she could not even have permission to confess to a priest. Father Corbe would have left at once, had not a violent fever hindered him. ... We decided to send Sister Cecilia and Sister Olympiade to care for our Mother and to console her. They took the stage the following morning...

"We continued our preparations for departure; already Sister Olympiade had put in a large bag all the important papers and the little money that we had, so that our Mother might have them when she left for another diocese. ..."

While the sisters were preparing for an unknown future, Father Corbe submitted his resignation as superior of the Congregation to Bishop de la Hailandière. The bishop replied, "I don't know why you wish to leave the diocese. It is up to those who confused things to remain to disembroil them. I received a letter from Terre Haute; I am sending it back unopened." Sisters on mission also sent letters to the bishop, and they, too, were returned unopened.

Just as all seemed lost, Providence intervened. Bishop de la Hailandière received a letter from Rome addressed to "Monsignor Bazin, Bishop of Vincennes." The Church had accepted Bishop de la Hailandière's resignation and appointed another bishop for the Diocese of Vincennes. Bishop de la Hailandière appointed Father Corbe to oversee the Sisters of Providence Congregation; and Father Corbe immediately sent word to Mother Theodore to return to Saint Mary-of-the-Woods.

Speaking of the "day of our deliverance," Sister St. Francis Xavier wrote: "That same day our mother had prevailed over Sister Cecilia and Sister Olympiade so that they finally agreed to visit the bishop. Monsignor reproached them for having delayed so long to come to see him and told them that they were going to be very happy that he was leaving Vincennes. Sister Cecilia replied, 'Monsignor, we will not rejoice at your leaving, but we will be happy to enjoy a little peace.' He gave them a letter for Sister St. Vincent. This letter announced that Father Corbe would be completely in charge of the Sisters of Providence until the arrival of Monsignor Bazin. His Lordship added that our conduct obliged him to make this decision.

"As soon as this excellent letter arrived here, we went in procession to Father Corbe to inform him of his acquisitions. He accepted the gift with the best grace in the world. We went immediately to the chapel to sing a hymn of thanksgiving in honor of the Blessed Virgin. The men, who were very happy, accompanied us and then began to unpack their traveling bags. The following Thursday, about six o'clock in the evening, our Mother arrived. We all thanked our Lord together, and this good day ended with Benediction of the Blessed Sacrament."

A time for rejoicing

The return of Mother Theodore to Saint Mary-of-the-Woods on June 10, 1847, was celebrated by the people of Terre Haute, for they, too, had grown to love and respect her. She traveled up the Wabash River on the steamboat Daniel Boone, arriving in Terre Haute at six o'clock that evening. Father Lalumiere, the priest at St. Joseph Church had arranged for the city's cannon to be fired to herald her arrival. As Mother Theodore neared Saint Mary-of-the-Woods, the workmen announced the approach of her wagon by firing their guns into the air; and a procession of sisters and postulants hurried to greet her. It was a moment of great joy and hope.

In July, Mother Theodore wrote to the bishop of Baltimore, Monsignor Samuel Eccleston, to tell him of the recent events and to thank him for his kindness to the sisters. She also wrote to Mother Mary: "I had been ill for almost two months with a heavy cold which left me not a moment's repose. I was, in addition, very tired, having traveled over seven hundred miles in five weeks. All this, joined to a great inquietude about the future of our community, had robbed me of almost all my physical strength. Monsignor's commands struck the final blow. ... Two days later I was dying. I sent for the vicar general; he refused to come. At midnight they found me so low that they sent to Monsignor's to ask for his nephew, whom he ordained last year and who is now pastor of the cathedral. He had the kindness to come and hear my confessions. ... I had always hoped that during the month of May the Blessed Virgin would not fail to send us some help ... I had been banished; illness alone kept me in Indiana. ... I was ill, without asylum, without money, without protector; the month of Mary was approaching its end; it was May 30..."

The trials were not at an end. In response to a flurry of rumors that Bishop de la Hailandière would remain in Vincennes to assist the new bishop, Mother Theodore wrote to Bishop Bouvier: "It is infinitely painful to me to come to afflict your heart again with the recital of our new sorrows; they believe here that only you can lighten them by writing in our favor to Monsignor Bazin. I confess that I am afraid nothing can cure our woes if it is true, as Monsignor de la Hailandière says publicly, that he is remaining with Monsignor Bazin to direct with him the Church of Vincennes. ... Two weeks ago Monsignor de la Hailandière took back all the rights he had abandoned in favor of our superior and deposed Father Corbe. He told our sisters in Vincennes again that he wishes to hold an election and that he will make the unworthiness of our conduct known to his coadjutor and that both of them will make us get back into line. He does not want to have "a country girl to govern a community," and the rest. He wishes to have "another congregation of submissive daughters who will have the spirit of God. ...

"The consecration of the new bishop will be held in the Church of Vincennes the twenty-fourth of this month, so when you read this letter it might well be that your poor daughters of Indiana have been dispersed like the dry leaves of their forest. ... I must tell you with difficulty, my good Father, that this time I feel myself overwhelmed; my soul is weary of struggling in vain against insurmountable difficulties. I see only abysses on both sides. ..."

Bishop Bouvier, true father of the Congregation that he was, evidently already had taken steps to safeguard the Sisters of Providence, for in a letter dated October 21, Mother Theodore sent him a message filled with good news and gratitude: "It would be difficult for me to tell you all the happiness your excellent letter brought us. The good God will reward you for the good you have done for the poor orphans of the woods. He alone can. This good God does not condemn our conduct, since it is approved by your Lordship and our dear mothers of Ruillé. All that we have suffered disappears in this greatest consolation. ... Our superior just received a very kind letter from Bishop Bazin; he assures him that he has no prejudice against us and that he will receive none, that he will pray much to heaven to enlighten him, and that he will act only for the glory of God. ... He said that he would ask nothing of us except that we follow our Rules. ..."

Mother Theodore was ill and unable to attend the consecration of Bishop Bazin on October 24, 1847. A few days later, he wrote her a short message, which said, in part: "... Bury the past in oblivion or think of it only to bless the Providence of God who sent you crosses because he loved you; for God never fails to try his true children. ... The future is yours. I shall judge you only by the future and according to your Constitutions." In late November, she received another letter from Bishop Bazin: "Your father having learned that you are better, and desiring that you will soon be completely restored, hastens to send you a letter from the bishop of Le Mans that he received this morning.

"Yes, good Mother, the wishes and hopes of the holy Bishop Bouvier will be realized; I hope that you will always find in me a father, a confidant, a friend in Jesus Christ to whom you will be able to confide without fear all your cares. You will feel my authority only as a support to help you have your Rule observed in all its perfection. A bishop should be for a superior who has the spirit of her state a lever to help her lift her heaviest burdens, a lamp which enlightens her in her doubts, and a confidant to whom she can confide her troubles and in whom she finds the consolation of which she has need. ... I believe that Monsignor de la Hailandière is leaving tomorrow by the stage; his belongings left yesterday by steamboat. ..."

In December, Mother Theodore sent to Bishop Bouvier a letter of gratitude and prayer for all that he had done for the Congregation. She also said, "The tribulations which have afflicted our community have produced very precious fruits. Besides the admirable union that exists between persons of different nationalities, of dispositions so opposite, some well informed, others without education, there is also among the sisters a great spirit of faith, of piety, and a confidence in God which goes as far, I believe, as it can go."

The priests and sisters who suffered under Bishop de la Hailandière put the past behind them and looked only to the future. They regarded their former bishop with compassion. In telling Father Corbe about Bishop de la Hailandière's departure from Vincennes, Bishop Bazin said, "... this good bishop is truly to be pitied. Like Don Quixote he tilts against windmills. He even imagined that I was influenced against him by bad advisers, that I listened to his enemies, etc. ... I pity him more than I blame him. … May God be with him and bless him." To Mother Mary, Mother Theodore wrote: "We pray for him daily, and I beg you, my dear Mother, not to forget him. He will be much higher in heaven, I am convinced, than if he had remained bishop."

It was finished.

7

Responding to the Needs of the Day

*We are not called upon to do all the good possible, but
only that which we can do.*

Mother Theodore Guerin

John Stephen Bazin, who ministered in missions in Alabama
before being named Bishop of Vincennes, directed the diocese
with a welcome blend of competency and spirituality. Under his
guidance, the turbulence of the past gave way to a sweet and
gentle calm. As priests and sisters rejoiced and settled into the
unfolding peace, no one was more grateful than Mother
Theodore. One of Bishop de la Hailandière's final acts was to
approve the Sisters of Providence Rule; and, within the first
weeks of his administration, Bishop Bazin gave the
Congregation a valid deed to the property at Saint Mary-of-the-
Woods. Now, finally, after years of struggle and heartache,
Mother Theodore could devote all of her energy to building and

nurturing the Congregation, to establishing schools and to sharing, by word and example, the love of God.

Joy and sorrow

The spring of 1848 was filled with activity. Work on the farm kept everyone busy. In a letter to Bishop Bouvier, Mother Theodore said: "... We seem to be among the prodigal sons, for our Indiana is covered with pigs. We salted twenty-five last week, and we have fifty for next year. ... It is our turn this year to pay a high price for bread. We pay two and a half cents a pound for flour, and we must have a great deal to feed our seventy-two persons here in the woods. Our school is our only source of income, and half the pupils do not pay us. ... We have several sick sisters, among them Sister Mary Xavier, who is suffering from inflammation of the lungs. ... As for myself, I have never been such a helpless creature, but, too, I have never been almost fifty years old."

Mother Theodore was heartened by Bishop Bazin's charitable works and entered eagerly into various projects with him, including opening a free pharmacy for the people of Vincennes. Historians record the beginnings of the pharmacy: "Sister Olympiade drew upon her stores of medicinal herbs, the virtues of which she had quickly learned from her pioneer neighbors, the mullein and pokeroot, the calomel, mint and horehound, which could be found in the woods at any time, and the senna, pennyroyal, elder blossom and sassafras root, which must be gathered in season. Carefully tied in bunches, they hung from the beams of the little log pharmacy at Saint Mary-of-the-Woods to be dispensed to the sick of the countryside and used as needed. Now she set aside a generous store for Vincennes, and on March 22, she left with Mother Theodore and Sister Joachim to prepare the pharmacy and to remain for a few days..."

In April, Mother Theodore again left Saint Mary-of-the-Woods, this time accompanied by Sister Mary Cecilia, for the annual visits to the establishments. The sisters traveled first, by steamboat, to Vincennes where Mother Theodore assisted at Bishop Bazin's Mass and received Holy Communion. Unaccustomed to the harsh cold of winter in Indiana, the bishop was suffering from exhaustion and a lingering cold. Nevertheless, he spent six hours in the confessional that Saturday. The next day, Palm Sunday, he was very ill. On Holy Saturday. Mother Theodore was called to bleed the bishop.

She wrote to the sisters at Saint Mary-of-the-Woods, "I have no more hope of saving him. ... I have just spent a few hours at his bedside. He spoke to me of you all, for his thoughts are upon our Congregation. He said that the doctor still hopes to save him, but I have not hope. God grant that I am mistaken." At seven o'clock that evening, after receiving the last sacraments, the bishop spoke to Mother Theodore: "Assure all your dear sisters that I tenderly love your Congregation. If I were to live longer I would not spare any sacrifice for its prosperity, spiritual and temporal. Assure them that such was my intention." Mother Theodore remained with the bishop throughout the night, praying while she tended his needs. Bishop Bazin died in the early morning of Easter Sunday, April 23, 1848.

Mother Theodore wrote of the loss to Bishop Bouvier: "It is almost in the light of the funeral tapers burning near the mortal remains of Bishop John Stephen Bazin, that weeping I trace these few lines to you. ... He is dead, this venerable prelate who in six months had healed so many wounds, and whose loss inflicts such a deep wound in the hearts of all those who have known him, but more particularly in those of his poor daughters of the woods whom he protected with such paternal kindness. ... How God tries our poor diocese! What will become of it? Nevertheless, we shall not cease to hope, for he who has protected us with so much love dies not. He will still protect us. ..."

It was the fervent hope of all that the Reverend Maurice de Saint-Palais, vicar general and administrator of the diocese, would succeed Bishop Bazin. Seven months later, he was named the bishop of Vincennes.

After the death of Bishop Bazin, Mother Theodore traveled on to Madison and then to Fort Wayne. Back at Saint Mary-of-the-Woods, she began collaborating with Father Lalumiere of St. Joseph Church in Terre Haute to build a school, which was to be known as St. Vincent's Academy. Father Lalumiere was to purchase a site and open a subscription to raise funds, while Mother Theodore was to build and operate the school.

In June, Father Lalumiere secured the lot; and in August the Sisters of Providence Council agreed to the plan, even though it meant the Congregation would have to borrow money. In the minutes of that meeting, Mother Theodore wrote, "In the hope that we might fulfill the end of our sublime vocation, we accepted the conditions ... namely to supply the remainder of the cost and other improvements, and to furnish the house and school ... The revenue from this house, as from all the others which we have established, will be our trust in Divine Providence."

The election of 1848

That summer of 1848, after careful consideration and hours of prayer, Mother Theodore announced that an election would be conducted during the annual retreat. This, the Congregation's first election, was necessary Mother Theodore said, "to put some organization into our poor little enterprise." The Congregation was growing at such a rate that it was nearly impossible for her to handle everything by herself. Her health was failing, and she continued to think about retiring as superior general of the Congregation.

In a Letter Circular to the sisters, she explained: "Notwithstanding the trials through which it has pleased our Lord that we should pass, he has deigned to bless our Congregation. It has grown in the shadow of the Cross, which still covers it … It is time to begin to organize ourselves, as much as possible, according to our Rule and Constitutions. My duties have multiplied to such an extent that it is impossible for me to fulfill them. I feel deeply the need of sharing a burden which I can no longer carry alone … I come to beg you to choose from among you a sister who has the spirit of her state and your confidence to give me as my first assistant. Another office, not less important, that of mistress of novices, must also be filled."

During the retreat, the sisters selected Sister Mary Cecilia as first assistant and Sister St. Francis Xavier as second assistant and mistress of novices. The sisters gave to Mother Theodore the four-inch white cross once worn by Mother Mary, superior general of the Sisters of Providence at Ruillé. Previously, Bishop de la Hailandière had declared that Mother Theodore could not wear the cross.

The work continues

Even as the sisters were returning to their missions after the retreat, work began on the establishment in Terre Haute. On August 28, Mother Theodore wrote, "Our men went with the oxen to haul the brick to begin the house at Terre Haute." Father Lalumiere supervised the work, which was fraught with repeated delays, and Mother Theodore often made the trip to the building site to direct and encourage the workers. After overseeing the construction of additions to the Academy at Saint

Mary-of-the-Woods, she was not without expertise — and she knew the skilled and dependable workmen and the best prices for brick, stone and labor.

The winter of 1848–49 set in early, with cold and snow in November, followed by heavy rains in December. The Wabash River was flooded and, for a time, Saint Mary-of-the-Woods was isolated. In November, Mother Theodore wrote to Sister Basilide at Madison: "I thought I could tell you many things this morning and write you a long letter, but I am compelled to leave at once for Pottsville and to go from there to Terre Haute. I cannot express to you all the trouble that the house in Terre Haute is giving me. It is not advancing rapidly, yet we must open school there in a few days. Pray God to bless it."

The "day school for young ladies," as it was advertised in the Wabash Courier newspaper, originally was scheduled to open in November, but construction was not yet complete in mid-December. Regardless of the weather, Mother Theodore was determined that the school would open the first of the year. Twenty-eight young girls were present when St. Vincent's Academy opened on January 2, 1849.

The enrollment was smaller than Mother Theodore hoped, but she was not discouraged. She was confident the school and the town would grow. "It is certain that the town of Terre Haute will become one of the largest in Indiana on account of its location," she wrote to Bishop Bouvier. "They are already making railroads, canals, doing away with the obstructions in the Wabash which prevent the passage of steamboats and so forth. They do here in one year what in the Old World would not be done in ten."

In the meantime, the diocese was preparing for the consecration of Bishop de Saint-Palais. Mother Theodore wrote to Bishop Bouvier, "God has given us the one whom the whole diocese has earnestly asked for since the death of Bishop Bazin.

… He made his studies at St. Sulpice, where he was ordained. It was there that he became acquainted with Bishop Bruté, who brought him to his poor mission of Indiana. He had been working here for twelve years with zeal and success. … It was he who came from Madison two years ago and brought over on the ice and snow of a rigorous winter our poor Sister Mary Liguori, who was in a dying condition."

Mother Theodore arrived at Vincennes a week before the consecration of Bishop de Saint-Palais, which was celebrated January 14, 1849. The river again was flooded, preventing several priests from reaching Vincennes. An epidemic of cholera along the Mississippi and Ohio rivers kept other clergy and bishops from attending. In a letter to Bishop Bouvier, Mother Theodore described a storm that battered the town of Vincennes: "On the day of the consecration a torrent of sleet fell. This is of frequent occurrence in America and forms a layer similar to molten lead, or lava from a volcano, covering every object it falls upon and taking its form. Woe to the man or beast exposed to its violence."

A week later, she returned to Saint Mary-of-the-Woods: "… in open wagons and with horses roughshod. They made particles of this polished surface fly up and go rolling on the ice, shining in the sun with a thousand colors. One might have fancied the horses were trampling under foot millions of precious stones and that we were traveling in an enchanted country. The enchantment, however, was only for the eyes. … We broke down four wagons, and finally our horses took fright four miles from Terre Haute and exposed us to the greatest danger. We were preserved only by a special protection from heaven."

In the same letter, she shared news of the Congregation, "Our Congregation is everywhere appreciated. Sisters are called for in almost every town of the diocese. … Our house in Terre Haute is not yet finished, although the sisters have been there a month. They have over fifty pupils and, it is said, will have more in the spring. If we had thirty sisters more, ready to go out, we could employ them all."

The cholera, which started in the coastal area of Louisiana, spread up the rivers to the Midwest. In July of 1849, Mother Theodore wrote to Bishop Bouvier, "You will be happy to hear that until now we have been spared. The epidemic is terrible all around us. … At Madison our schools are closed and the sisters are employed in taking care of the sick at their homes. …"

Scattered outbreaks of cholera continued through the summer of 1850. As they did in Madison, sisters also cared for the ill and dying in Fort Wayne and Vincennes. At one point in Madison, eight people died in two days. Concerned about the welfare of the sisters ministering in Madison, Mother Theodore instructed them to practice extreme cleanliness. Even though it was Lent, she ordered them not to fast, but to eat well-cooked, wholesome foods. She added: "Be cheerful and amiable toward one another; have nothing on your conscience to cause you uneasiness. … Finally, my dear daughters, pray. … Pray as much as your occupations permit."

For the children

When Mother Theodore visited the establishment at Fort Wayne in the spring of 1849, she met the orphan children of Miami Indian heritage who were attending the school. Her heart was captivated. Later, she wrote, "The children at Fort Wayne wept when I left them. I too felt like crying. All are Catholics, the majority having received Baptism at our school. … I love them very much. … I longed to be a mother to them."

Bishop de Saint-Palais, too, was touched by the needs of the children in Indiana, so many of whom were orphans. "God bless me," he often said, "these little ones must never suffer want or neglect." He turned to Mother Theodore and the Sisters of Providence to care for the children at two new orphanages in Vincennes.

That summer, Mother Theodore sat down at her writing desk for a visit with Bishop Bouvier: "Although there is nothing remarkable to communicate to your Lordship, I feel none the less the desire of having a little chat with you, knowing you will be happy to learn that your daughers of the woods continue to enjoy the peace so long awaited, so ardently desired. ... There are always from six to seven hundred pupils in our schools. About two-thirds are Catholics. ... Several who have been educated in our houses, and are now married and in society, are advocates of our holy religion. We begin to see the good which our Congregation is doing in this country. Nevertheless, we must expect to suffer much here, surrounded by those who are interested in many ways of destroying or at least weakening, our influence. ... For three or four weeks the heat has been suffocating. When there is no breeze at all, one can scarcely breathe. The heat is due, I believe, to the drought. At Saint Mary-of-the-Woods, it has rained hard only once since the last days of April. Yesterday we had a heavy rain, which did great good to everything."

In November, Mother Theodore wrote to France: "We have a large number now of poor little orphan girls at Vincennes for whom there is no resource save the Providence of God who feeds the birds and causes the grass to grow. Are they not dear to his heart? ... Our good bishop is now making the visitation of his diocese, and he himself solicits charity for these little girls. There are five still here with us, but we will keep them as they will not be received at the asylum after the age of ten, and ours are older than that."

The need for orphanages was great. Nearly a year later, in September of 1850, Bishop de Saint-Palais asked Mother Theodore also to care for orphan boys. She agreed and dispatched three sisters to minister to thirty little boys. By this time, too, the sisters were caring for forty-seven girls.

Joy and awe

The winter of 1849 was so severe that, at times, the stage could not plow through the deep snow covering the road to Saint Mary-of-the-Woods. In February, Mother Theodore accompanied a sister who was ill to Vincennes to see the physician there. Upon returning to Saint Mary-of-the-Woods, Mother Theodore developed pneumonia. For the next several weeks, she was able to manage her correspondence and direct the activities on the farm, but she did not recover until March. Realizing how fragile her health was becoming, the sisters and Father Corbe counseled her not to take long trips by stage or steamboat, especially during the winter months.

The toll of the years was evident in Mother Theodore's appearance and bearing. The fevers which returned each winter left her increasingly weak and frail. She survived on a light gruel and a soft mixture of flour and milk, occasionally seasoned with squirrel broth. Physical suffering aside, Mother Theodore's zealous spirit and twinkling sense of humor remained as strong as tempered steel. She was blessed with an innate and constant ability to experience feelings of joy and awe in the world and its people.

That spring, during her tour of the establishments, Mother Theodore stopped in Louisville to purchase supplies and pianos for the schools in Fort Wayne and Madison. She returned to Saint Mary-of-the-Woods in time for the harvest, which began in mid-June and continued into the early fall. During harvest, she worked in the gardens, fields and orchards alongside the workmen and sisters. One hot and humid day while they were working in the hay field, Mother Theodore paused, wiped the moisture and sticky chaff from her face and said, "O my God, you will keep an account of this."

Mother Theodore never tired of the unfolding seasons in the Midwest: the furiously magnificent thunderstorms, the dust-laden droughts, the captivating, crystal sleet, the snow falling silently in the forest, the raging floods. On many occasions, seeking peace and solitude, she slipped quietly into the forest. "We discover anew every time something grand, useful and beautiful in the great forest of Indiana," she wrote. "At each step one marvels at the grandeur, the power and goodness of our God. How generously he has provided for our wants, I would almost say, for our pleasures."

A new motherhouse

Bishop de Saint-Palais long had been concerned about the condition of the old farmhouse that served as the sisters' motherhouse at Saint Mary-of-the-Woods. After participating in the retreat during the hot summer of 1850, he put his desire to build a new motherhouse into action. Mother Theodore wrote, "This good bishop is always devoted to us. He suffered very much during the retreat at seeing us so poorly housed. ... We were crowded together with the sun darting its burning rays upon us. The heat was stifling. ... What grieves me most is to see Our Lord so poorly lodged and our sick sisters in a common dormitory where the beds almost touch one another under a plank roof."

The bishop was quick to bring his proposal for a new motherhouse to the Sisters of Providence Council. With the bishop's promise of financial assistance, the Council agreed to the plan and, before September, Mother Theodore signed the first contract with the quarry at nearby Pottsville for stone for the building's foundation.

Mother Theodore's excitement about the new building was tempered by her dread of debt and by unsettling conditions in the diocese. In December, she wrote to France, "Our schools have suffered much this year from Protestant opposition. There are now only thirty-three pupils at the Academy. Moreover, several of the Catholics do not pay. We are as poor as Job. It is impossible to think of building. Bishop de Saint-Palais gave us four hundred dollars last month to purchase materials, but I was obliged to use it to buy provisions which are almost all half again as dear as last year. ... The pupils being less numerous in the establishments, also, our income has diminished. ... All things considered, we will have to remain as we are for it is impossible to build this year. ... We have been ten years in our cabin. With the help of God we can live there a little longer."

Still, the winter was mild, and Mother Theodore began gathering building materials. The workmen built a brickyard and a kiln and cut wood for fuel, and the first brick was fired in July. Preparations for the actual building of the house continued throughout the long, hot summer, memorable because Bishop de Saint-Palais began a journey to France that would last sixteen months.

By January of 1851, the workmen were hauling stone from the quarry over frozen roads. Friends of the Congregation were contributing gifts to help with the cost of the new facility, but expenses were rising steadily. Mother Theodore wrote, "We are beginning to build a house which will cost more than fifty thousand francs, a terrible undertaking for little persons like us. I feel my courage slipping away at the thought."

The building was to be simple: a three-story brick structure with basement. When the first sod was turned in May, Mother

Theodore recorded the joy of the moment in a letter to Mother Mary: "Since we have been on this side of the ocean, whenever anything extraordinary has happened to us, my first thought is usually for God, my second for you. … Last Monday, the day consecrated to honor our beloved Blessed Mother under the title Help of Christians, a feast restricted, I believe, to America, the excavation for the foundation of our future chapel and house was begun. Five men are working with machines and six horses which quickly carry off the earth to a little distance. We wish to have a basement under the entire house, six feet beneath the floor timbers. It will cost three hundred dollars more, but will give solidity to the building, and will assure coolness in the summer and prevent frost in winter. Weather permitting, we shall have the cornerstone laid on the last day of this beautiful month of May, although I fear that the rain may interfere with our plans. …

"You will pray for us, will you not, my Mother? God has facilitated the work thus far; we have only quiet and industrious workmen, and a continuance of such circumstances will give us much to be grateful for. We have, however, one terrible obstacle to the work — water and mud, and great breaks of frightful size in the road from here to Terre Haute."

When the cornerstone was blessed by Father Corbe on June 13, 1852, the feast of Corpus Christi, Mother Theodore's prayer, as recorded in the community diary, was simply this: "My God, grant that all those who live and die within these sacred walls may be good religious, saints." When the sisters returned to Saint Mary-of-the-Woods for their retreat, they were greeted by the sight of the walls of their new home, now two-thirds finished.

In July, Mother Theodore wrote to Bishop Bouvier: "… We could manage very well if our motherhouse were built and paid for. We have very few debts now. They would all be paid off this year if we did not have to build. But it becomes absolutely necessary to build. We are literally piled upon one another, which is not only inconvenient, but very unhealthy during the extreme heat of the summer. And the heat is excessive this year. Every day we have storms, rain, etc. Our brick makers are quite disconcerted. At this moment the sisters are haymaking, because with so much rain the hay is spoiling. A storm the last night of April destroyed all the fruit in this part of the country. Even a large number of the trees were blown down. ...

"Then there came a large swarm of locusts which made terrible ravages in our orchards. Our forests themselves look like vast orange groves, on account of the numberless little tender branches which have been cut down by these insects and now, having become yellow, are hanging down, from afar resembling oranges. The locusts are something like the May bug; we know not whence they come. They are armed with a kind of saw which is dangerous, not only to plants but to animals, and even to man. They make a sort of buzzing noise during the whole time of their existence, which lasts only five or six weeks. Then they die, after having deposited, one knows not where, the seed for another generation, which fortunately is not developed until seventeen years later; but they never fail to reappear after that time. ...."

When Bishop de Saint-Palais returned to Saint Mary-of-the-Woods in October, he was pleased to see forty men working on the motherhouse, which was nearly ready to roof. By June of 1853, a dozen sisters were preparing to move into the dormitory as soon as the freshly plastered walls were dry. As the expenses of finishing the house grew, Mother Theodore's confidence in Providence remained steadfast. "Providence has succored us in a remarkable manner during the past year. Never did a workman come for his wage without my being able to pay it. I have paid out, including this year, twelve thousand dollars, sixty-three thousand francs. ... We have paid fifty thousand francs for our motherhouse. Our debts yet standing are from twenty to twenty-five thousand francs."

Early in July of 1853, Mother Theodore sent a Letter Circular to the sisters calling them to retreat. She said: "By the help of God and the union which reigns among you, a house is here to receive you. As yet it has only the walls and roof with scarcely any furniture; but such as it is, you will love it, for it is the fruit of your labor and privations. …

"When we compare the little frame house in which we were received in charity twelve years ago with the splendid building erected here now, we clearly see the effects of those powerful words, 'Increase and multiply.' Indeed, my sisters, we have increased and multiplied. Our exterior improvements are astonishing; but does our interior advancement correspond with the exterior? … Come, then, my dear daughters, to refresh your souls alone with your God. … Our little chapel will be blessed by the bishop on the sixth of August. I hope all will be here for the solemnity. Remember to be, on your way home, models of reserve and modesty. May your Guardian Angels preserve you from all evil…"

In July, the workmen carefully placed a gilt globe and a cross in the cupola of the new motherhouse. For Mother Theodore, who despaired at the lack of crosses atop churches in the United States, it was a moment of joy. She reflected: "The world was saved by the Cross. Glory and honor to it. How consoling to a Christian heart to see it raised on high in the New World. O my God, grant that it may triumph."

Now the sisters hastened to prepare the new chapel, which ran the length of the eastern side of the building. The sisters lined the tabernacle with white velvet. In the niche behind the altar, they placed the beloved statue of the Madonna, a gift in 1841 from Perrault de la Bertaudière, a friend and benefactor of the Congregation.

Sharing the news of the new chapel with her former superiors in Ruillé, Mother Theodore wrote, "We will send you a picture of the interior as soon as we can make one. The chapel is nicely ornamented. … It is the prettiest little chapel I have seen anywhere since I left France. Though so beautiful, it is nevertheless very simple. We will send also a picture of our house with this letter. … It is said to be the most beautiful building in the state."

In April of 1854, when Mother Theodore received word that Bishop Bouvier was sending a portrait of himself to the Sisters of Providence, she wrote a lengthy letter in which she thanked him and reflected about the Congregation's years and progress in Indiana. "When you sent your six daughters to Saint Mary-of-the-Woods, you thought they were going to lay the foundation of an establishment which, later on, would be of service to religion; but with the means you made use of — these persons, so poor in every respect, strangers to the country, the customs and the language of the New World — you never expected to see the fruits of your zeal crowned with so much success.

"Today we are eighty persons in our community, sixty-four, including twelve novices, wearing the religious habit, and sixteen postulants. There are nearly a thousand children in our schools, eighty-five boarders here at the Academy, thirty-seven of whom are Catholics. …

"At last they have finished painting our house. The painters are here in my room now, interrupting with their questions. I find the house too fine; it gives me great uneasiness about my vow of poverty. It looks more like a castle than the house of poor little Sisters of Providence. I think it might have been built cheaper and made less elegant. I wanted only simplicity, and I do not know how elegance has come in, in spite of myself. How unhappy I should be if, through my example, extravagance would be introduced among us. This thought takes away from me much of the pleasure I have in seeing my sisters well lodged and their house finished. The last doors were hung on Holy Saturday, which tells you how much we have suffered this winter in this large open house. …

"We have the consolation now of seeing Our Lord more suitably cared for in our chapel, which is pretty well ornamented for our woods. The chapel does not give me scruples as the rest does. You see, my Father, your prayers for us to God have been heard."

In truth, the house was lovely, elegant in its simplicity. Coal oil lamps and candles provided light, and the heating system consisted of fireplaces and a few small stoves. Water and wood were carried from the outside to all three floors of the building. Furnishings were minimal. The bricks of the house were painted a soft gray hue; the shutters, a dark green.

Bishop de Saint-Palais and Father Corbe blessed the chapel on Sunday, August 7. Mother Theodore prayed, "O my God, grant that all who dwell in this house may love thee much, may love one another, and may never forget why they came here. Grant that we may all be reunited in Heaven."

8

An Enduring Love

*No one will ever love you as your old
Mother Theodore does.*

Mother Theodore Guerin

In all that she did in her life, Mother Theodore was inspired by love. Her vocation itself, like a rose bursting into bloom in the warmth of the spring sun, was a manifestation of her love for God and for the Catholic Church. Her love was so powerful that it enabled her to overcome what otherwise would have been daunting hardships. Because she loved God and knew that God loved her, she found the strength and the grace to persevere. Because she loved God, she also loved people and accepted them as they were, even while encouraging them to grow into their full potential and to live loving, virtuous lives. Because she loved, she was able to forgive, even those people who persecuted, betrayed and ridiculed her. Her entire life reflects that love, for it permeated her every action, word and deed. That powerful, forgiving, enabling love was especially evident during the final years of her life.

A pioneer in education

Throughout her years in Indiana, Mother Theodore was a pioneer in providing opportunities for education. For more than a decade, from 1841 to 1852, the Academy at Saint Mary-of-the-Woods was the only Catholic boarding school for girls in Indiana. Prior to 1840, two private academies and one public school for young girls existed in the state. In an attempt to help parishes establish schools for their children, Mother Theodore, from the time of her arrival at Saint Mary-of-the-Woods in 1840 to January 1849, established parish schools at Jasper, St. Peter's, Vincennes, Madison, Fort Wayne and Terre Haute, all in Indiana, and at St. Francisville in Illinois. In 1853, she opened establishments in Evansville and North Madison; in 1854, at Lanesville, a small town in south central Indiana; and in 1855 at Columbus, located south of Indianapolis. Additionally, with Bishop de Saint-Palais, she established two orphanages in Vincennes. As Mother Theodore's stature as an educator — and that of the Sisters of Providence — developed, and as they became more widely known, enrollment in the schools increased steadily. The Congregation depended on the income from the schools, but they accepted — and cared for — students who were unable to pay.

In 1850, the Indiana Legislature set aside funds for a system of free public schools and established the Office of the Superintendent of Public Instruction to oversee the schools, teaching methods and textbooks. With the advent of public education, enrollment in the sisters' schools dropped off, but only a few months passed before the students began returning to the Catholic schools. Mother Theodore's letters to Bishop Bouvier at Le Mans and to the superiors of the Sisters of

Providence at Ruillé reflect the changes that were taking place in Indiana.

In June of 1849, she wrote to Mother Mary: "At Vincennes we have four sisters and about a hundred pupils, among whom there are very few Protestants. There are thirty in the school called 'paying' and seventy in the free school. ... At Madison we have five sisters and about one hundred and thirty pupils, one class of Catholics and the other of Protestants. ... At Jasper we have more than one hundred children, boys and girls. Nearly all are German. This establishment barely sustains itself but does much good by instructing the Catholics. ... At Fort Wayne we have five sisters. ... We have one hundred and twenty pupils there, of whom twelve are boarders. ... At Terre Haute we already have four sisters and eighty pupils. ... At Saint Mary's we have thirty-two or thirty-three boarders, and we have also twenty to thirty children in our free school at Saint Mary's, which makes in all our schools about six hundred children. ... The Protestants lose their prejudices in our classes, and their parents also; everywhere we go, they come to seek us, to see us, to speak with us. All are proud to have us in their houses. ..."

When Mother Theodore corresponded with Mother Mary in February of 1852, she included information about the school in Madison: "This very morning I have received letters from Sisters St. Vincent and Basilide. Both are well. The Protestants of Madison are opening school after school. ... They wish to make us pay taxes, which is contrary to the laws of the state. We refuse positively. It embarrasses them a little to have women resist them and speak to them about the law. Woman in this country is only yet one fourth of the family. I hope that, through the influence of religion and education, she will eventually become at least one half — the 'better half.' "

Mother Theodore's concern about the increasing number of public schools and the subsequent drop in the enrollment in

Catholic schools was apparent in a letter to Ruillé in 1853. "We are told that next year we shall not have a single Protestant pupil," she wrote. "These public schools have already caused our Protestant classes at Madison to fail, and they even threaten the Catholic classes; but we have offered to teach the latter for nothing rather than let them go to these schools. ... We are poor, but the Heavenly Father will feed us. He would not let us die of hunger. Pray for us and for our poor Catholics so unjustly persecuted."

Early in 1854, Mother Theodore wrote to Bishop Bouvier: "... They have obtained a new law which orders a general tax for the purpose of educating all the children in the same schools without distinction of sex and fortune. These schools now in vogue throughout the Union have closed all the others, with very few exceptions. The Catholic schools are nearly the only ones remaining open, but the attendance is much smaller than in the preceding years, especially in some localities.

"We have always a fair number of Catholic children. The two new establishments at Evansville and North Madison are prospering. Between them, they have over two hundred pupils. ... We have at Fort Wayne eighteen boarders and one hundred and fifty day pupils. ... Our boarding school here at Saint Mary-of-the-Woods is also well attended — seventy-eight pupils.

"But what most consoles us is the good that is being done here. Not only are there always several receiving instructions for Baptism, but there are many Catholics who are learning to know and serve God. The Catholics of this locality have for the past thirty years seen a priest only once a month, in passing, and some even only once a year. They are Christians, yet for the most part, very ignorant, scarcely knowing what is absolutely indispensable. Their daughters, brought up in our school where there is, I may say, a good spirit, return home like little apostles.

... You would be consoled could you see the fervor and piety of these young girls. ... This year we have over thirty Catholic boarders, which shows you the prosperity of the country. Ten or twelve years ago there were not ten Catholics in Indiana who could pay for the board and tuition of their daughters, even for six months; at present a large number are able to give them a good education. ..."

A group of anti-Catholic citizens known as the Know-Nothings contributed to the hardships experienced by the Catholic schools. The Know-Nothings feared the religion and the influence of the pope and the bishops. They were alarmed at the rapidly increasing number of Catholic immigrants in the United States; and they resented the growing prosperity of the Catholics. Mother Theodore described the potentially dangerous situation in a letter to Ruillé in March 1855: "... Last year, especially, they organized against the Catholics an infernal association which, in a month or two, covered the face of America like a flock of sparrows. They call themselves Know-Nothings, a name which they took in order to envelop their abominable designs in mystery. They swear by the most frightful oaths to destroy all that pertains to the Catholic religion. Murder, deceit and all the horrors at which an honest soul trembles are the means they promise to employ and which they swear to practice at the peril of their lives. In one of the Indiana newspapers, they wrote that I am a tyrant, an abominable monster who keeps young girls against their will in our house, which they call a tavern or haunt of brigands. ... For several days we thought they were going to come to burn us alive. Well, we are still living, but we do not know for how long. May the will of God be done!"

Mother Theodore corresponded frequently with Sister Basilide, who was ministering as superior of the school in Madison. Many of the letters were devoted to counseling and consoling Sister Basilide, who was apt to make hasty decisions.

In March of 1855, in response to Sister Basilide's anxiety about the drop in enrollment at Madison, Mother Theodore offered words of comfort — and advice: "I wish to say a few words to you, to tell you that I indeed share in your trouble. It is in fact very painful to see the number of your pupils diminish each day. You have seen your Protestant pupils disappear one after another; that was a terrible blow. ... Now you must see your dear Catholics abandon you also. ... Take courage, my daughter; pray, pray much for yourself, for your establishment, for that city. Submit yourself to what the good God will wish to ordain, and try not to let these household contradictions influence your relations with your companions; that is not asking a little. It is very difficult and requires rare virtue not to make others share what we are suffering. I have not yet found in my Basilide that wisdom which asks of each one only what she can give. ... Do you remember the fable of Lafontaine, which speaks of the animals who were going to wage war, how their king knew how to make use of each one's talents and to employ each one according to its instincts? The talent of a good superior is to do the same, to ask of each one only what she is able to give. ... Believe me, my daughter, always and everywhere you will find people who will try your patience, and you will try theirs — except in Heaven."

In the end, the Know-Nothings and the public school system could not destroy the Catholic schools. Within months, Catholic and Protestant parents alike began returning their children to the schools administered by the Sisters of Providence. The curriculum offered in the public schools could not compare to that of the Catholic schools and, too, the presence of the Sisters of Providence in the daily lives of the children was of great and lasting influence.

Woven of love

With love and grace, Mother Theodore wove individual women into the Congregation. She handled each one with care, taking into consideration each woman's strengths and weaknesses. Nowhere is this more evident than in the letters she wrote to the sisters who were on mission. In between the annual visits and retreats, letters were the only way Mother Theodore had of keeping in touch with the sisters, of understanding what they were enduring, of teaching and guiding them, of sharing their burdens and accomplishments. For the sisters living at home at Saint Mary-of-the-Woods, the hour of five o'clock in the afternoon was devoted to instruction. At that cherished hour, the sisters gathered to listen to Mother Theodore. Always, she urged the sisters to remember: "Charity must be the beloved virtue of the Sisters of Providence..."

When Sister Mary Xavier was adjusting to her new ministry at the orphanage in Vincennes, Mother Theodore wrote to her: "Remember that you have not only to teach them how to sew, but also how to become meek, humble and patient; and this kind of lesson is given much better by example than by precept. Be obedient, and, above all, be patient. ... Poor little ones, how dear they should be to you. ... Love all in God and for God, and all will be well. ..."

Sister Maria was plagued with feelings of self doubt. Mother Theodore counseled her in numerous letters, and, finally, in January of 1856, she wrote: "You do well not to miss your Communion anymore. When we are cold, that is not the time to keep away from the fire. ... We must always correspond to the grace of God to the best of our ability, not through fear of sin, but from a sentiment of love. ... Thank you very much for my woolen skirt. I think that it will do very well. Have confidence in God, peace in his arms, no worry and no fancies, and you will find happiness."

Mother Theodore encouraged Sister Mary James with these words: "In the morning say to yourself, 'My God, here is yet a day given to me to love and serve you.' Be glad of it, offer him all your actions, your temptations, your little humiliations, and go to your duties with cheerfulness."

Always concerned about the well-being of the children, Mother Theodore often reminded the sisters to treat them gently and with respect and love. In January of 1856, she wrote to Sister Veronique: "Be sweet and kind with the little girls. ... You can do them much good or much harm. These children will never forget what they have seen you do. ... I thank you for saying the chaplet of the Immaculate Conception in thanksgiving. I pray you to continue it. I say it myself every day. Let us pray for one another, so that the few days which remain for us to live may be employed in serving the good God, in gaining souls for him. ..."

One of the reflections she shared with her good friend, Sister St. Francis Xavier, was simply this: "Is it not astonishing that after all that he has done for us, we still do not know how to abandon ourselves without reserve to his guidance!"

In 1852, when the Congregation was anticipating the arrival of a group of postulants from France, Mother Theodore wrote a letter of greeting to them and told them a little of what they could expect to experience in Indiana: "... He calls you to this foreign land watered by the sweat and blood of so many holy missionaries who came before you to make known, served and loved the God who has chosen you. ... One cannot belong to God in an imperfect way and be happy here. ... If your heart wavers, if you fear the Cross, poverty, humiliation, do not leave France. ... The Lord will help you, he will protect you, he will be your guide during the long and painful voyage, he will lead you into our dear forest where you will find sisters who love you already, who are praying for you, to whom you are already very dear."

The conferences Mother Theodore presented for the sisters at Saint Mary-of-the-Woods usually focused on the Rule, spirituality or teaching methods. On teaching children, she said, "Oh what a beautiful vocation is ours! Have you sometimes thought that you are called to do on Earth what our Lord himself did? He instructed, and you instruct. He was surrounded by little children, and you, you spend your lives among them."

In June of 1848, she spoke to the sisters about Jesus: "... But Jesus always has time, he is always ready to listen to us. You know, my dear sisters, when we had left our country and all that was dear to us, we found beyond the sea a friend, a Father. We found waiting for us in a poor long cabin our God, our all. Yes, it was near him that we consoled ourselves for all our privations. And since then he has never left us; he shares our miserable dwelling with us. He remains with us day and night. Yes, while you are peacefully sleeping, Jesus is watching over you. ... He continues to exercise the same vigilance over us that he showed for his apostles, which so touched the heart of St. Peter. ... 'Jesus was like a mother to us,' said the prince of the apostles to his disciple, St. Clement; and I say to you, my dear sisters, that Jesus in the Sacrament of the Eucharist is as tender and vigilant for us as he was for his apostles. ..."

Is it any wonder that the sisters loved Mother Theodore?

And the years pass

As the years passed, one after another, Mother Theodore continued managing the Congregation and its farm, visiting the establishments, and corresponding with sisters and friends in the United States and abroad. Increasingly frail, ill for long weeks at a time, she moved through the years at peace with her God.

The winter of 1854 was extremely cold, resulting in misery and sickness among the people of Indiana. A chilly, rainy spring was followed by a summer of intense heat and drought. Mother Theodore was ill during the late winter and into the spring, but when smallpox was reported in Terre Haute, she crossed the river to vaccinate the children, thus protecting them from the dreaded disease.

When she returned to Saint Mary-of-the-Woods on June 3 after visiting the establishments, she found the crops on the farm withering and dying in the intense heat. As the drought consumed crops and gardens in the midwestern states, the cost of food increased dramatically. Because the supply of corn — a staple food — had dwindled to nearly nothing, some of the livestock on the farm had to be slaughtered.

Mother Theodore wrote to Bishop Bouvier: "We have a sort of famine in the United States. All provisions are expensive as gold. Potatoes are sold at an exorbitant price at New Orleans; everything else is dear in proportion. The wheat and potatoes failed entirely this year on account of the drought and the excessive heat we have had to suffer this summer. The heat also is considered the cause of the terrible maladies which under different names have decimated the United States."

The forests and fields were dry and brittle that summer. Late one afternoon, when Mother Theodore was returning from Terre Haute, she saw flames and smoke billowing in the forest not far from the buildings at Saint Mary-of-the-Woods. Arriving at the farm, she scrambled from the wagon and ran to assemble workmen and sisters into a firefighting brigade.

A Sister of Providence historian recorded the event: "As soon as they reached the woods, they divided into groups near the burning trees, scattering and throwing back toward the original flames the blazing leaves on the ground by which the fire was approaching the farm buildings. They all worked for over an hour, up and down the deep ravines and through the woods. It was now growing dark, and the forest fire was burning less fiercely. Gradually the groups began to assemble. ... All were finally accounted for except Mother Theodore, and the clear voices of the novices calling her through the woods brought no answering echo. ... Finally Jean, one of the workmen, mounted to the summit of a hill and began to call with all his might. A faint, faraway voice responded, and in the distance a moving light appeared. It was indeed Mother Theodore. Seeing that the fire was dying away, she had gone to the farmhouse for a lantern and returning had lost her way. For three-quarters of an hour she had been sitting alone on a log in the woods resigned to pass the night or even a longer time there. ..." During those dusky, smoke-filled hours, a light rain began to fall and continued through the night, dousing the flames in the forest at Saint Mary-of-the-Woods.

On September 12, 1854, Mother Theodore traveled to Lanesville to establish the new mission there. From Lanesville, she and Sister Basilide started out for Madison. During this journey an accident occurred that some believe hastened the death of Mother Theodore. The steamboat on which the two sisters were traveling was to arrive at Madison during the night, and the crew had been asked to summon the sisters to disembark. The sisters were forgotten, however, and there was nothing for them to do but continue on to the next stop, where they boarded the first steamboat headed back toward Madison. Too late, they discovered that the boat was not scheduled to stop at Madison. Seeing the sisters' dilemma, the captain agreed to transport them to shore at Madison in a small rowboat.

The Ohio River, seldom a gentle river, was swollen, turbulent with autumn rain. As Mother Theodore and Sister Basilide stepped into the boat, it shifted and both sisters fell into the cold angry water. Sister Basilide was rescued immediately, but Mother Theodore was in the water several minutes, clinging with one arm to a piece of the steamboat. As soon as she was safe, the men from the boat took the sisters to the convent in Madison. Both sisters, who were wearing long, heavy habits, were soaked to the bone. Mother Theodore was suffering from shock and exposure. Though she returned shortly to Saint Mary-of-the-Woods, she did not speak of the accident and only mentioned it briefly in her diary. The Congregation was not aware of what had happened until the following summer when Sister Basilide returned to the motherhouse.

When Mother Mary Cecilia wrote about the life of Mother Theodore, she said: "Mother's health was failing. Every year we saw her weaker and more ailing but ... she omitted none of her duties. She visited the missions, enduring the fatigues of traveling and, at that time, not only fatigue but real hardships, as a good deal of the route was made by stage over very bad roads. ... Mother had a strong physical constitution (though it was undermined by wretched health), and moral courage to a high degree. With the fortitude that grace gives, she would probably have lived for several years longer, bearing up against a suffering body and still managing the affairs of the community and directing its spiritual government, but for the accident on the river. ... Disease settled itself ... to its work of death. ... The impression made on Mother was so terrible that she did not mention it when she returned and never spoke of it to anyone. She came home worse than usual, it is true, but we were so used to seeing her sick that we did not suspect any particular cause. ... From this date, Mother's poor health changed for much worse. During the fall and winter which followed this accident, she was so disabled that she could not attend to affairs as she had always done."

Ill though she was that fall, Mother Theodore recorded in the diary a special event: "On the night of the seventh to the eighth of October, the silence of our forests of Saint Mary's was greatly disturbed by the whistling and puffing of the steam engines which passed Saint Mary's for the first time on the way to Paris, Illinois. The road is not finished, nor will it be for six months; nevertheless, the cars go by Saint Mary-of-the-Woods every day."

Then in December an occasion of great joy occurred. On December 8, 1854, the solemn promulgation of the decree of the dogma of the Immaculate Conception was announced in Rome. Devoted as she was to the Blessed Mother, Mother Theodore had long awaited this news. Word did not reach Saint Mary-of-the-Woods, however, until January 13, 1855, when Father Corbe read it in the French newspaper and announced it during his sermon. For Mother Theodore and the Sisters of Providence, the day became one of celebration, given to ringing the convent bells, singing the *Te Deum* and adorning statues of Our Lady, which were displayed in places of honor throughout the Academy and convent, with lights and flowers.

Enduring love

The beautiful dawn of 1855 soon gave way to loss and sorrow. During this year, Mother Theodore mourned the death of her friend and confidant, Bishop Bouvier, the bishop of Le Mans. She also witnessed the physical weakening of other loved ones, including Bishop de Saint-Palais. Though Bishop de Saint-Palais continued traveling the vast Diocese of Vincennes, he was suffering from colds and pneumonia and recurring bouts of malaria and rheumatism.

In a Letter Circular dated February 10, 1855, Mother Theodore announced the death of the bishop of Le Mans: "… He died in the Eternal City after having heard from the mouth of the successor of St. Peter–Pope Pius IX — the decree of the Immaculate Conception of our Blessed Mother — a decree which he had desired all his life. His heart was full of gratitude and consolation, but his happiness was a celestial joy. ... 'It is good to die here,' he said. ... Our community is indebted to him for its Rule and Constitutions. Saint Mary-of-the-Woods owes to him its very existence and preservation. This saintly and learned prelate was for us in our days of darkness what the cloud was for the Israelites in the desert — a shelter and a light. In our days of peace he was ever a father. Five weeks before starting on his great and last journey, he sent us his portrait, expressing his regret at not being able to come himself to his 'beloved daughters of the woods.'..."

In March, Mother Theodore wrote a long letter to Sister Athanase, who had been her companion in the novitiate at Ruillé: "Here I am, completely exhausted and still unable to take care of business, after an inflammation of the lungs which kept me for two weeks in bed or near it. I can write today, and I am profiting by it to come and chat with you. That which one does with pleasure, does not tire one so much. ...

"I do not forget my well-loved companions of Ruillé, particularly those who have, like me, seen pass over their heads, already whitened by age, the miseries and the worries of life, of so many winters. ... O how fortunate we are, my very dear sister, to have given the days of our youth to that God of love who gives us so much affection, and even more when we are old, infirm and crippled than when we were young and robust. ... It matters little whether we are in one place or another, provided we do the will of God. I do not doubt that if our superiors had chosen you in my place, you would have accepted to come to America, and you would have done it in a less imperfect manner than I; of this I am well convinced. But no, they would never have consented to make the sacrifice of losing you. ...

"It was not the same for me. I thank the good God from the bottom of my heart for having wished to make use of an instrument so vile, so contemptible, to do some good in our dear mission. … The good God always makes use of nothing in order to accomplish something. He builds on nothingness. … It has pleased him to cause a great work to grow in the shadow of the Cross. We are seventy-four sisters wearing the religious habit. We have, besides, eighteen postulants. All the sisters are occupied with teaching; we have in all more than one thousand pupils, of whom about two thirds are Catholic; and these poor Catholics would have no religious education if the sisters did not give it to them. The Protestants, especially those in our boarding school, all leave as Catholics or nearly Catholics, at least in their hearts. … Each year several are baptized, and at this moment six are being prepared for Baptism.

"…I have to laugh at your privations of wine. If you had been here for fifteen years, you would not know whether there was still wine on Earth, except for the Holy Sacrifice. … We also have cholera, dysentery and the whole family of evils which afflict the human race. Now, we are stricken in the chest; the winter is so long, so cold and so severe that it will not leave our woods without making some lungs tuberculous. One of our dear sisters is in the last stages of consumption; the other, or rather several, are beginning…"

The strength that Mother Theodore usually found with the coming of spring did not return in 1855. In June, she wrote in her diary: "We leave with the bishop for Vincennes. I cough all the time and go to consult the doctor. … I return on the second of July very feeble. A novena was made for me to the Blessed Virgin, Mary Immaculate. … The sisters and children united and said special prayers. It is to the favor of the Virgin Immaculate that I owe my improvement. Oh, my Mother, obtain for me the grace to profit by my state of suffering, and to draw from it all the benefit that your divine Son expects from it for his glory and the good of your little community of the woods."

On July 8, 1855, Mother Theodore prepared a Letter Circular calling the sisters home to retreat: "... the longed-for time of our annual retreat has come once more. The voice of the Lord calls you to your dear solitude of Saint Mary's, not only that you may rest after a year of painful labors, but especially that you may purify your hearts more and more in communion with God, and acquire new strength and fervor for the time to come. Put everything in good order in your establishment and in your employments, and come as soon as possible to give me the consolation of seeing you all, fervent and united, which is the greatest happiness that I can have in this world."

Such was Mother Theodore's enduring love.

9

In the Presence of God...

Continue to walk in the presence of God, to do your actions solely to please him, and to bear courageously all the trials which he may permit you to have.

Mother Theodore Guerin

Mother Theodore loved her Sisters of Providence. She cherished the time spent in retreat when they all gathered at Saint Mary-of-the-Woods to pray and rest and enjoy one another. She anticipated the visits to the establishments because then she could linger with individual sisters and share their spiritual and personal joys, sorrows and concerns.

Mother Theodore did not hide her affection for the sisters. In a letter to Sister Basilide she once remarked, "The name of Mother is not given in vain. Could I forget what you are to me? No, no one will ever love you as your old Mother Theodore does. ..." During one of her many journeys away from Saint Mary-of-the-Woods, she wrote, "You understand at least, my dearly beloved sisters, that I do not have to get down deep in my heart before finding the tender love that fills it for you all." Upon returning from the long visit in France in 1843, she wrote, "After almost a year of separation, of anxieties and of sufferings, I saw them all again. Imagine our feelings when, with emotion too deep for words, we went to kneel before him to whom we owe all our happiness. Before Jesus who so lovingly watched over us we could pour forth our hearts."

Though Mother Theodore had long anticipated the retreat of 1855, she was not able to participate in it. When the missionary sisters returned home to Saint Mary-of-the-Woods that summer, Mother Theodore was not waiting to greet them. Her physician had ordered her to rest in bed. It was the beginning of the end.

In a brief diary entry dated August 6, Mother Theodore wrote: "Eleven novices were professed. Six of our postulants received the habit, and four professed sisters took perpetual vows. Monsignor, assisted by our Father Corbe, presided at the ceremony. Sister Mary Cecilia replaced me for my part in the ceremonies."

But when the retreat was finished, Mother Theodore wrote to Mother Mary in Ruillé, and in that letter she opened her heart: "I neither die nor live. One week I am a little better and the next I relapse. ... The sisters came to the retreat and are leaving today for their missions without my being able to say a word to them although they have been here six weeks. The feast of the Assumption, the day on which the retreat closed, and the day that eleven novices took their vows and six postulants received the habit, it was absolutely impossible for me to assist in any way. ... You can see now, dear Mother, that our Lord wished to make me see the truth of what you told me — that I was very proud and foolish to think that my sisters still had need of me, as everything passed off perfectly without my having a hand in it at all. I do not doubt but that it will be the same when I shall have closed my eyes. I have said so to myself many times, but I did not know it so clearly as after the experience I had. ...

"A pilgrimage to St. Anne d'Auray was promised for me, and since then I am a little better. ... But my chest is always very bad, and for several days past my cough is worse. I am fully convinced that it is only by nothing less than a miracle that I shall see the end of the winter. I am resigned to the holy will of God; in fact, I feel even nearer to him since I am continually on the Cross. This long agony is a favor of which I was not worthy. ..."

On August 22, Sister St. Francis Xavier, who was Mother Theodore's first assistant, wrote to Bishop Martin in Louisiana to tell him about Mother Theodore's condition and to ask for his prayers: "In our poor exile, days of joy are more often anticipated than realized. We had hoped this summer to enjoy a little of our Mother whose health all winter had been so bad that she scarcely left her room. Well, Father, this summer she is worse than ever. She started out to visit the missions and fell sick again at Fort Wayne. Since the month of May, Mother Theodore is merely living. Doctor Baty says her heart is failing. ... I have firm confidence that God will leave her to us. I do not ask that she may be as strong and active as formerly. Oh, no! May he only leave her to us! Only leave her! Dear Father, pray for us, pray for her — as you love us!

"...Most of our dear sisters were here for the retreat. They came and went, at least the majority, without getting to say a word to Mother. How they wept in bidding us farewell! ... For the first time, Mother could not be present at the reception. And while her daughters were pronouncing their vows, she was upon her couch. You can imagine how grieved we were. Saturday morning, Father Corbe took Holy Communion to Mother. ... Today Mother is somewhat better; so I have come to talk with you a while, to rest myself a little. ..."

That fall, Mother Theodore wrote to tell Mother Mary that the Rule had been translated into English, but that she would not have it printed in English until she received word that the French Rule had been approved by Rome. "If you have any hope of the Rule being approved before long, please let us know soon," she said. Then, she confided, "… It has been proved that I have an incurable heart disease which threatens me with instantaneous death. Ask for me of the good God that it be not unforeseen, and that I be always ready to say to the Lord when he calls me, 'My God, here I am.' "

Hope

In September of 1855, after regaining a little strength, Mother Theodore resumed her duties: the endless correspondence, the tasks and decisions associated with directing the government of the Congregation, and the cherished five o'clock conferences. Her work was not finished.

For years Mother Theodore had harbored a desire to build a beautiful chapel in honor of Mary, the Mother of Jesus. Now, with renewed energy, she began plans to gather building materials, to have the brick fired and the stone quarried. She asked Mother Mary for a copy of the plans that were being used for the church that was being built at Ruillé.

On October 22, the anniversary of the founding of the Congregation, Mother Theodore wrote in her diary that she had signed the contract to have the brick burned for the chapel in honor of the Blessed Virgin: "… Today, fifteen years ago, she brought us to our woods and has ever since protected us. What joy to erect a monument to her!"

The anniversary was a time of profound reflection for Mother Theodore. Alone in her room, she must have spent hours pondering the years, for on the inside cover of one of her ledgers, a book of financial accounts, she penned a summary of those fifteen years along with a message of inspiration for the Sisters of Providence. On that ledger cover she wrote:

"Glory to the most Holy Trinity: Father, Son and Holy Spirit.

"Honor to Mary, conceived without sin.

"In you, O Lord, I have hoped; I shall never be confounded.

"Yes, my dear daughters, hope in God, and you will not be confounded. See what he has already done for you. Fifteen years ago today, October 22, 1840, six sisters arrived in this forest, at that time so savage; they were strangers to the country, to the manners and customs, to the ways of America; they did not know one word of English. Now we are a community composed of sixty; here at Saint Mary's we are eighteen sisters wearing the religious habit, and twenty postulants ardently desiring to be clothed in it.

"More than twelve hundred children receive religious instructions in our twelve houses of education which already bear abundant fruit. What good is being done by the sisters of Saint Mary's! What good remains for them to do, if they are faithful to their holy vocation!

"The spiritual good is not the only favor which it has pleased God to bestow on us. We were received in our woods by charity. Joseph Thralls, whose name will always be in the prayers of the Sisters of Providence, sheltered under his roof those who, like their Divine Model, did not have a stone on which to lay their head. Now the Academy has been built for a long time; the improvements, which have rendered Saint Mary's a charming place, have been made. We have bought the lot in Madison for three thousand dollars. We have built the house in Terre Haute and its schools; improved our establishments in Fort Wayne, Evansville and, finally, we have built and paid for our beautiful motherhouse.

"There, my children, is what the Good God has done for you — for fifteen years what he has done for you in the midst of crosses and afflictions of all kinds. This, a thing essential to a religious community, has remained intact in ours. I mean the union … a tender charity has constantly existed among us; you have shown it, this holy charity, this union of hearts, especially in our days of trials. Where does one ever live a union more strong and more genuine, more general? There is, my dear daughters, the secret of our strength, the firm foundation of our prosperity, the source of our success. Do you always want to succeed? Always to add to the glory of God, to strengthen the Church, to raise a large family of saints, to be as happy here below as it is possible to be? Continue to love one another. Remain attached as you are now and as you have been to your superiors, to your Mother, to your loving God. If it is thus, you will be happy in time and in eternity. I promise it to you from the side of God. Your devoted Mother in Jesus Christ, Our Lord. Sister St. Theodore. Pray for the repose of her soul."

Quietly, in the solitude of her room, Mother Theodore was finishing her tasks. Surely, she knew that her life on Earth was soon to end.

In October, in an attempt to fulfill a fifteen-year-old promise, she wrote to Sister Basilide: "… As usual, I shall speak to you without reserve. When I wrote you the ninth of this month that my heart was turning toward France, I did not pretend to insinuate that I wished to return there. No! On the eighth of September fifteen years ago, the day when for the first time we received our Divine Savior in this land of America, it ceased then to be for me a foreign land. It became my land of adoption; and there, under your own eyes, in the church of Brooklyn, I took the vow of living and dying here, unless obedience directed me otherwise. Since that day, not a thought, still less a desire, of seeing France again in order to remain there has come to trouble my soul, even in the most stormy days!

"It has not been the same with you; you have always looked back on that dear fatherland with a certain regret for having left it. I did what I could to persuade you not to look back, and to make a great and generous sacrifice to God. You have done and undone it many times. Poor Basilide! You are so wanting in constancy and firmness. The reason, it seems to me, of this inconstancy in your character is, partly, that you permit yourself to listen to nature's voice; you are not dependent enough on the spirit of God. Age does not change us much in this particular; only the habit of recollection and the spirit of faith in all our actions will effect this change. Be that as it may, you still have the desire of returning to France? Well, my daughter, I shall keep my promise — you may return if you wish. I promised the same to all the others before we embarked.

"I feel now that my life is very near its end, and before I die I want to say again what I said to you fifteen years ago: If you wish to return to France you may do so. ... Reflect seriously on what you desire to do; above all, pray much that our dear Lord may make known to you what he wishes you to do. If you decide to go, the money will not be wanting. ... Good-bye, my dear Sister Basilide. I am going to offer my prayers for you that the Holy Spirit may inspire you and lead you, and the Blessed Virgin protect you."

As fall gave way to winter, the plans for the church had not yet arrived from France. So, in December, Mother Theodore again wrote to Mother Mary: "All the sisters of Saint Mary's, especially all those who have had the privilege of knowing you, united in offering to you their wishes and their homage; also to ask a favor of you, hoping to obtain it as it would be for the glory of our good Blessed Mother. You will not refuse it. It is this. You know, Mother, that we would like to build a chapel. We should have to be our own architect and surveyor. We entreat you then, dear Mother, to send us the plan for your church, or, if you think it would not be suitable in our woods, would you have the kindness to have one made by the person who made yours or by someone else? We would like it in Gothic style, at least one hundred feet long, width and length in proportion. We could select the most appropriate place for it, as space is not wanting here. ... Kindly give your attention to this matter as soon as possible, if you please. As to the expense, we shall immediately remit the money upon learning what the amount will be."

While Mother Theodore awaited a response from Mother Mary, she went ahead with preparations and ordered ten thousand feet of ash flooring for the chapel and forty cords of wood to be used to burn the brick for it.

A season of winter

The winter was snowy and so cold as to be "almost unbearable," Mother Theodore said. Regardless, just after Christmas, on December 28, the Congregation celebrated the feast of St. Theodore–Mother Theodore's patron saint. In her diary, Mother Theodore wrote: "Our feast of St. Theodore was very pious and full of gratitude to God and our Immaculate Mother. Also to St. Anne for the favors she had obtained for us."

A letter written by Sister Maurice Schnell added details. Sister Maurice noted that the community room was decorated for the occasion with a painting of the Blessed Virgin, the cherished portrait of Bishop Bouvier and a statue of St. Anne adorned with a crown of flowers. Sister Maurice added, "Father Corbe, Mother Theodore, Sister St. Francis Xavier, Sister Mary Cecilia and Sister Olympiade sat in a nice little row" during the evening's entertainment of music and French dialogue.

All too soon, however, the joy of December gave way to despair. Sister St. Francis Xavier, in poor health for many years, was ill. In her diary, Mother Theodore wrote: "January 23 —

Sister St. Francis Xavier falls ill of a nervous disorder which causes her unheard-of sufferings in the right side of her chest, in her neck and in her head. January 24 — Today the invalid has a violent fever. This fever and the pains do not change, except to redouble. My God, save her for your glory and our good! January 27 — This is for us a day of crosses, afflictions and trials. My God, may your will be done! Our dear invalid received the Last Sacraments."

While Sister St. Francis Xavier was dying, one of the workmen, Père Michel Guthneck, who was the father of three Sisters of Providence, died. In the diary, Mother Theodore wrote, "He has been here for twelve years, working with the greatest devotedness. He has gone to receive in heaven the reward of his work, of his love for the community, and especially of the Christian virtues which he practiced like a saint."

As she stood by the window in Sister St. Francis Xavier's room and watched Père Michel's funeral procession pass by, Mother Theodore knew the death of her friend and trusted first assistant was drawing near.

When Sister St. Francis Xavier died, Mother Theodore stood strong and courageous before the Sisters of Providence. "My dear sisters," she said, "since we have a sacrifice to make, let us make it generously and not yield to immoderate grief."

She did not attempt to hide her sorrow when she wrote to Mother Mary and Mother St. Charles in Ruillé: "Our very dear, our beloved Sister St. Francis Xavier is no longer of this world. She was taken from us the last day of January after an illness of eight days. ... The loss we have sustained is immense — you know that well. Sister St. Francis was the soul of our Congregation. She gave it her spirit, and upheld it by her exhortations, her letters, her prayers, and by her example. For me in particular, she was a friend that one does not lose twice in a lifetime. She filled the void left in so many instances by my failures. She encouraged me by her example and good counsels; she reproved me for my faults with a charity and courage which my brusqueness and my haughty and imperious character had never discouraged; in a word, she was everything to me. Her death leaves me, as it were, alone in the midst of the community. ...

"I did not think, neither did the sisters, that in my poor state of health I could survive this dear sister. I could hardly sit up when she fell sick, and, during the last four days, I scarcely left her at all day or night. I asked of Our Lady only that I might live long enough to close her eyes when she would die. Then I asked to live till she was buried; finally, I prayed Our Lord to let me live long enough and enable me to issue the Letter Circular and write to you. More than that I have asked nothing. ...

"I am bringing Sister Mary Cecilia to the motherhouse, and we must necessarily begin to organize a house which, up to this day, has been managed by Sister St. Francis and myself. A new era is about to begin for this Congregation; but, I repeat it, I hope it will be an era for its progress and its well-being. ...

"For seven weeks Terre Haute has been covered with a heavy fall of snow; very fortunately, however, for without that, the vegetables, flowers and even the trees would be frozen. They are carting wood on the Wabash River. ... Our bishop was two days coming here from Vincennes last week. ... Ice is everywhere."

Weak and grieving, Mother Theodore continued corresponding with the sisters on mission and conducting the five o'clock conferences for those at Saint Mary-of-the-Woods. And, as always, she found moments to marvel at God's handiwork. Looking out her window early one morning at a frost-covered world, she wrote, "This gives to our forest an air of purity and innocence very pleasing to the sight. What will heaven be if our poor Earth is at times so beautiful!"

On March 2, she moved Sister Mary Cecilia, who had been ministering as superior of the Academy, to the motherhouse to serve as her assistant and to guide the novitiate. Mother Theodore's great anxiety during these, the final weeks of her life, was concern about who would replace her as superior general. To Mother Mary she wrote, "If I only had, as you say, a person to replace me. But there is none. And I do not know where to find one to train her. All these considerations have thrown me into a deep sadness. … You will blame me, no doubt, for not having provided against the contingency sooner. I blame myself; yet it seems to me that I could not do anything about it. …"

The chalice of suffering

On Palm Sunday, March 16, 1856, the Sisters of Providence ministering in Terre Haute returned to Saint Mary-of-the-Woods for a Holy Week retreat. Mother Theodore participated in the Mass, but the next day she became ill and left the chapel. Later that day, she asked for her diary, and in it she wrote: "I am obliged to keep my bed. What a beautiful week to be upon the Cross. O good Cross, I will love thee with all my heart." These were the last words she wrote.

On Easter Sunday, Sister Mary Joseph Le Fer de la Motte wrote to the Sisters of Providence in France: "Good Mother, the chalice of suffering is not yet drained, and after having had the sorrow of seeing our beloved Sister St. Francis leave us, we have the further distress of seeing our dear Mother about to be taken from us. This good Mother fell ill almost two weeks ago, and the illness showed the symptoms of her ordinary intestinal inflammations; the doctor said that it was a congestion. Is it more dangerous? I do not know. …

"On Good Friday night, our Mother sent for me; she was so weak, so very weak, Sister Olympiade found her weak enough to die. This dear Mother asked me to write you when she was no longer with us; but her request can well be complied with during her life, for if she were to live twenty more years, her feelings for you would always be the same; hers is a heart which does not change. 'You will tell our Mothers how much I love them, and that if I die it will be in communion of heart and mind with our dear congregation of Ruillé. I have never for a moment ceased to love our superiors. …' "

Mother Theodore died during the early morning hours of May 14, 1856. In the community diary, Sister Mary Cecilia wrote: "Mother dies at a quarter past three a.m., the life, the all of the community!"

On May 17, Sister Mary Joseph wrote to Mother Mary to tell her of the death of Mother Theodore: "All is over! … Your daughters of Saint Mary-of-the-Woods no longer have a Mother! That heart so tender and so good is now without feeling. She does not see our tears, she does not hear our sighs, and she is no longer here to console us for having lost her! Who, then, will calm our grief? … Since we have become more than ever the daughters of Providence, it will not leave us unaided. …

"Our cherished Mother, our beloved Mother is at rest. … But had she not finished her tasks? Is it not now our turn to labor and to suffer in order to deserve to go to join her? When I think of myself, I weep; when I forget myself, I am consoled. …

"Yes, without a doubt the powerful hand which keeps the world in motion can enable some feeble instrument to further his work; but it is not every day that he creates a heart like Mother Theodore's, and he does not always add to goodness of heart the gifts of high intelligence, solid judgment, boundless devotion and peerless virtue. She did not grow tired of suffering, and when Sister Olympiade and I were bewailing the length of her illness, 'O my poor daughters,' she said. 'It is very short compared to eternity.' "

Sister Mary Joseph continued, "Our good bishop came himself for the funeral. Two of his priests sang the High Mass; our poor Father Corbe would never have been able to manage it. ... Our chapel was all hung in white with black teardrops and as many lights as possible, forty candles and torches. We had the consolation of bearing our Mother, coffin opened, to the cemetery. ... She is buried near Sister St. Francis, and we are going to place Sister St. Liguori on the other side of her, as she had wished.

"From where I am writing, I see the bricks for our new chapel. O Mother! The sight of them saddens me. We had received the plans Holy Thursday, and although she was already very ill, our poor Mother was rejoicing and, from her bed, was building a new temple to the glory of the Lord. ..."

Consolation and challenge

The task of writing the Letter Circular about the death of Mother Theodore fell to Sister Mary Cecilia, Mother Theodore's first assistant. She wrote: "... I feel unequal to the task of writing the memorial of our beloved Mother. I cannot do justice to it; little did I ever think it would devolve upon me. But I need not say much, for which one of us does not know the excellence of her who was our Mother for fifteen years. ...

"When we consider her many qualifications — her spacious mind, her admirable character and the precious qualities of her heart, we are embarrassed to know which we should admire the most. There was but one feeling, one impression with regard to

Mother Theodore. She commanded universal admiration and love; all those who saw her, whether Catholics or Protestants, seculars or persons in religion, rich or poor, all were struck with enthusiastic admiration at her superior merit. ...

"She possessed to an eminent degree all the virtues of Christian perfection, though charity did seem to transcend them all; it was her favorite virtue ... her instructions and recommendations breathed charity, unbounded charity, a charity involving all the other virtues. She blended the tenderness of a mother with the firmness of a superior so perfectly that her government, as you well know, was the most happy and effectual. ... She has left us a legacy far more precious and valuable than can be bequeathed by the most opulent; it is the example of her virtues, which I hope shall ever dwell in our remembrance, to admonish us if necessary, but always to invite and urge us to a like perfection. ...

"Remember, my dear sisters, that our duties remain the same; we have our God to serve, and to serve him in high perfection. Our Rule is as binding as ever; and our various employments must be performed with the same zeal and exactness. Let us then continue as we did under the guidance of our departed Mother, with a fixed intention of accomplishing the will of God in all things. ... Thus we shall follow the path she has traced out for each one of us, and we shall enter eternity by the same gate that she did. ..."

Mother Theodore's legacy

A large Celtic cross of stone memorializes Mother Theodore's grave in the Sisters of Providence Cemetery at Saint Mary-of-the-Woods. The five missionary Sisters of Providence who accompanied Mother Theodore to Indiana — Sister St. Vincent, Sister Basilide, Sister Olympiade, Sister Mary Xavier and Sister

Mary Liguori — rest nearby, along with the superiors general who directed the Congregation during the ensuing years.

The words etched in the stone of the cross seem to echo from deep within Mother Theodore's soul: "I sleep, but my heart watches over this house which I have built." For though Mother Theodore no longer walks the forest paths at Saint Mary-of-the-Woods and no longer is present to instruct the Sisters of Providence, her legacy continues, and an awareness of her presence is constantly evident. Mother Theodore lives today through the ministries of the Congregation she created and through new generations who hear her story and follow her example.

For the Sisters of Providence, Mother Theodore's tradition of responding to the needs of the day is the impetus for their ministries. In the light of that tradition, Sisters of Providence have developed ministries designed to enable illiterate adults to learn to read, to gain the equivalency of a high school education, and, ultimately, to improve their way of living. Ministries among the poor and those who are ill and dying also were born of that tradition, as are those that focus on child care and ways of encouraging non-violence and justice for all people. Still other Sisters of Providence maintain a vital presence in classrooms throughout the United States, ministering as teachers and principals. To further the work of the Church, Sisters of Providence minister in parishes and in Church administration.

Through the years of ministry, Mother Theodore and her Sisters of Providence of Saint Mary-of-the-Woods have touched tens of thousands of lives in the United States of America and in other lands, including Taiwan, China, South America and the West Indies.

For all people, Mother Theodore's life and virtues serve as powerful, unforgettable reminders that all things are possible with God. Consider ... at one time or the other, in many different ways, most people are exiles, struggling to find their way in unfamiliar territory. Most people, occasionally or frequently, are victims of prejudice and discrimination, taunted because of their age, nationality, religion, size or gender. Responsibility and hardships are part of every life. People who embrace Mother Theodore as a woman for our time, a woman of virtue, discover that she met each of the trials and hardships in her life with love, charity, acceptance, forgiveness and hope — always hope.

What would Mother Theodore say to the people of today who are hungry for peace, justice, comfort and reconciliation with themselves and with others? Gently, oh so gently, she would say to pray and to love one another. She would advise young and old alike to seek strength and sustenance in the Eucharist and to look to Mary, the Mother of Jesus, as a model of obedience, devotion and acceptance. She would repeat her advice that, "Unless nourished, faith like love becomes extinguished." She would say, her dark eyes sparkling with love and grace, "Put yourself gently into the hands of Providence. ... Love all in God and for God, and all will be well."

10

The Cause for the Beatification & Canonization of Mother Theodore

Pray for me occasionally that I may not lose courage; nay, more, that I may be brave enough to hold up others who falter sometimes.

—Mother Theodore Guerin

The Cause for the Beatification and Canonization of Mother Theodore Guerin began in 1909 when Bishop Francis Silas Chatard of the Diocese of Indianapolis approved the opening of the informative process, the first of a series of long and arduous tasks required to determine if a person is worthy of beatification and canonization. The informative process, which ended in 1913, included testimony from twenty-four individuals.

Unofficially, Mother Theodore's Cause began during her lifetime. During Mother Theodore's ministry in Indiana, many people—recognizing the love and holiness that permeated her actions—considered her to be a saint and to have saintly qualities. Mother Theodore's deep and everlasting spirituality was reflected in her eyes, in her gentle smile, in her presence.

So it was that the Cause of Mother Theodore, like that of any other person who attains beatification and canonization, evolved from a following of individuals who believed that she was a holy woman who now is in heaven with God.

A virtuous woman

People who knew Mother Theodore did not forget her. Each had a story to tell about her kindness, her love, her goodness, her devotion. A measure of the feeling she inspired in others is evident in the following reflections and testimonies.

Shortly after Mother Theodore died, Father John Corbe, chaplain of the Sisters of Providence of Saint Mary-of-the-Woods, wrote: "… The sisters turned to me, drawing me by the edge of my soutane, as if to seek consolation. Alas! There was none in my heart; I did not so much as know whether I had a heart, for my heart and my soul seemed paralyzed.

"The combat was then over, and the victory won; the extraordinary beauty which shone on the countenance of that good Mother proclaimed clearly that already God had glorified his servant. A reflection of that glory, I am sure, lighted her face, which became for a moment luminous and shining with purity and happiness. I had never seen her so beautiful, and in the midst of my sorrow and of that desolating scene, I could not cease to contemplate her with a secret consolation. She did not seem to me to be dead, but to be sleeping in the sweetest and most peaceful sleep. It is thus that the saints die, or rather, that they sleep in the Lord at the end of their beautiful lives filled with good works and virtues."

Brigid Kelly, who lived at Saint Mary-of-the-Woods Village, remembered: "When I thought I could not live in this wilderness, as it was then, Mother Theodore said to me, 'When you go out, pray, pray to the God of the mountains and the trees, especially when you are in the woods. When you are lonesome, pray to the good God. He was alone in the desert.' Mother Theodore was always a comfort."

Monsignor A. J. Rawlinson, a former chaplain at Saint Mary-of-the-Woods, believed that Mother Theodore was thought of as a saint because of her charity. Recalling the words of one man, he said, "This humble layman declared her a saint because he had seen her spending all her energies to provide for the temporal as well as for the spiritual needs of the religious committed to her care. He could give positive testimony that she had sought the poor that she might clothe them, that she might nurse them. And he knew that she had done all these things because she regarded the poor as God's special gift to herself. She sought no thanks from the poor because she felt that she was indebted to them for the inestimable privilege of providing for their wants. To her, each one of them was Christ himself. …"

In France, M. Léon Aubineau wrote: "… God sustained her, fortified her heart, lifted up her soul in proportion as her duties became more numerous and more delicate. … No one knew her without loving her, and no one spoke to her without carrying away an ineffable remembrance. We saw her only once, in 1843, when she came to collect alms in France; we are still, as on that first day, under the spell of that exquisite eloquence, of that grace, of that indescribable amiability, which is more than distinction and courtesy, which is the outpouring and the light of virtue in a happily endowed soul."

Sister St. Antoine Hermann spoke of Mother Theodore's ministry among the orphans at Vincennes: "I noticed her particular virtue was charity. I was edified and touched by the way she spoke to those poor children. She recommended them to be kind to one another, to love one another. ... Mother was an example for us by her perfect faithfulness to every rule. ... We were always very happy to be with her because she was so kind and encouraging; and the work was very hard in those days and the poverty great. In her presence we always felt something like a grace, a holiness coming from her. And she was so tender. Sometimes, when in the midst of our work, I would say, 'Mother, I am hungry,' immediately Mother would say to someone near, 'Get a piece of bread for that dear child, she is young and hungry.' Sometimes it was only a piece of dry bread and a cup of water that came, but it was sweeter than candy. And she looked at me with joy, seeing that I relished my collation so heartily. ... In Mother's spiritual direction, her first advice was 'love one another.' ... She spoke to everybody, and everybody wished to speak to her. On the streets, they followed her for a word of advice."

Sister Mary John Hetfield was a Protestant when she enrolled at the Academy at Saint Mary-of-the-Woods and first encountered Mother Theodore. Sister Mary John said, "There was something so pleasing in her countenance that we hailed her coming with joy."

Sister Ann Cecilia Buell, a former student at the Academy, remembered: "Her carriage was majestic, but her manner exceedingly benign. Her face was beautiful from kindness and joyousness of expression. I have been accustomed to tell my impression of her by saying, 'Whenever Mother Theodore passed me, I felt that a blessing had fallen on me.' "

Hugh D. Roquet of the Saint Mary-of-the-Woods Village neighborhood recalled that his deceased aunts, who knew Mother Theodore, "would often remark upon the piety and charity of Mother Theodore, saying, 'Had it not been for her pious efforts there never would have been a Saint Mary's.' She would visit the poor and sick and reckless, and advise and console and help them for their good. ... It mattered not what religion of the sick and needy; all were cared for alike by Mother Theodore."

Sister Mary Eudoxie Marshall, who arrived at Saint Mary-of-the-Woods in 1854, said, "She had the greatest reverence for the sovereign pontiff and all ecclesiastical authority. Among the saints, she had a special devotion to the Blessed Virgin, St. Anne and the Holy Angels. She remained firm in her faith until death and showed her great faith in all the trials to which she submitted. ... She was just in all her dealings. She never made workmen wait for their pay and was very conscientious in keeping contracts. She was never severe in her judgment of others, nor permitted others to be so. I never knew her justice to be doubted by anyone. ... She was firm when circumstances required it, but never yielded to anger. ... She never yielded to unjust demands when the rights of the Church or of her community were affected. No fear nor human respect ever made her give in to any injustice. ... During her life she was considered a very holy person. As far as I was able to note, she was considered generally as a saint. I do not know when her reputation for sanctity began, but it has continued. ... It is my opinion that her prayer and her intercessions have considerable efficacy with God."

Mother Anastasie Brown, who was a member of the Sisters of Providence Council with Mother Theodore, said: "She did everything for the glory of God. She had a firm faith that did not turn aside. She had a great love for the Holy Sacrifice of the Mass and inspired others with the same love. ... She showed great love for the Holy Scripture and did all she could to inspire others with this same love. ... Her faith remained firm until her death, and I have often heard her repeat in her instructions that she was ready to give her life for her faith. ... She was filled with hope and inspired the same virtue by her instructions."

Ten years after Mother Theodore's death, Bayliss Hanna, a United States senator who lived in Terre Haute, presided at the closing exercises at the Academy. At the conclusion of his address, he said, "The unostentatious tomb of Mother Theodore over yonder in this little village of the dead is unembellished with monumental significance, but the narrow path that winds its way there will every year become furrowed deeper and deeper by the footprints of the grateful pilgrims who will go there to do homage to the memory of the foundress of Saint Mary-of-the-Woods."

The process

An intense investigation into the life, ministry and writings of Mother Theodore followed the informative process. The investigation, which spanned several decades, was conducted by church officials in the Archdiocese of Indianapolis and by the Vatican's Sacred Congregation for the Causes of Saints. Mother Theodore's writings were approved by the Congregation for the Causes of Saints in 1927. In 1956, Pope Pius XII signed a document authorizing the continuation of the Cause.

In 1978, Sister Joseph Eleanor Ryan began compiling the *Positio*, a detailed, documented account of Mother Theodore's work and writings. The *Positio* contains letters written by and to Mother Theodore and accounts by Sisters of Providence and others who witnessed her work and her presence. The *Positio* was approved by the Vatican's historical consultants and theologians, and on July 22, 1992, Pope John Paul II granted the title "Venerable" to Mother Theodore in recognition of a virtuous and heroic life.

The next step in the Cause involved proving that a miracle occurred through the intercession of Mother Theodore. So it was that an intense study of the healing of Sister Mary Theodosia Mug began. (An account of the miracle follows.) The study included documentation of medical procedures practiced in Indiana in the early 1900s. During the winter of 1996 and the spring of 1997, medical consultants, theologians and cardinals affiliated with the Sacred Congregation for the Causes of Saints approved the healing of Sister Mary Theodosia, through the intercession of Mother Theodore, as a miracle. In July of 1997, Pope John Paul II accepted the healing as a miracle, thus clearing the way for the beatification of Mother Theodore. During a ceremony on October 25, 1998, Mother Theodore was granted the title "Blessed." Beatification is the term used to signify that Mother Theodore and other holy persons are in heaven and are worthy of veneration and honor.

In order for a Cause to advance, a second miracle, occurring after beatification, must be documented. Subsequently, a healing in 2001 through the intercession of Mother Theodore was selected for study.

Like the miracle healing of Sister Mary Theodosia Mug, the healing of Phil McCord had to be carefully documented for investigation by physicians, theologians and cardinals at the Vatican. On January 23, 2003, the Archdiocese of Indianapolis began a formal trial to determine the validity of the claims that Phil McCord's vision was restored through the intercession of Mother Theodore. From that day until April 7, 2003, when the trial formally closed, archdiocesan officials gathered testimony from the physicians who treated McCord and studied his medical records. Once compiled and sealed the testimony was carried to the Vatican, where it was studied for evidence that the miracle was, indeed, authentic.

In June of 2005, the Sisters of Providence received word that the commission of medical examiners appointed by the Congregation for the Causes of Saints at the Vatican could find no medical explanation for the cure of Phil McCord. The commission approved the cure as a miracle. In November of 2005, the commission of theologians, also appointed by the Congregation for the Causes of Saints, approved the healing as evidence of a miracle granted through the intercession of Mother Theodore. On February 21, 2006, the Commission of the Ordinary Congregation of Cardinals announced a "positive declaration" concerning the miracle. The commission presented a recommendation for the canonization of Mother Theodore to Pope Benedict XVI.

The next day, the Sisters of Providence announced the approval of the miracle during a press conference at Saint Mary-of-the-Woods. Sister Ann Margaret O'Hara, general superior of the Sisters of Providence, said: "I share this news with you as I stand beneath her portrait aware of her spirit alive in the Congregation. ... The Sisters of Providence and many who knew her have long regarded her as a holy woman. And today Catholic Church officials have given the highest honor of sainthood to Mother Theodore, the only person from Indiana so honored. While canonization is an honor in the Catholic Church, the way Mother Theodore lived is a model for people of all faiths."

On April 28, 2006, Pope Benedict XVI signed a decree acknowledging the second miracle, a healing attributed to the intercession of Mother Theodore, the final requirement for canonization. July 1, during a meeting of cardinals who work in Rome, the Pope announced that Mother Theodore and three other holy people would be canonized during a ceremony October 15, 2006, in Saint Peter's Square at the Vatican.

The first miracle

The life of Sister Mary Theodosia Mug is intricately entwined in the Cause of Mother Theodore Guerin. For it was the healing of Sister Mary Theodosia, through the intercession of Mother Theodore that—scores of years later—led to the beatification of Mother Theodore.

Sister Mary Theodosia, a teacher and a writer, was born in 1860 in Attica, Indiana. In the 1850s, her mother, Ellen Phillips Mug, attended the Academy at Saint Mary-of-the-Woods and received instruction for First Communion from Mother Theodore. Ellen was a student at the Academy when Mother Theodore died in 1856. Like her mother, Sister Mary Theodosia enrolled in the Academy. She graduated in 1877 and entered the Sisters of Providence Congregation the following January. Sister Mary Theodosia professed perpetual vows August 15, 1891.

While a young woman, Sister Mary Theodosia suffered from neuritis in her right hand and arm. Neuritis, an inflammation of the nerves, causes intense pain. In 1902, she was too ill to teach, and the Congregation sent her to Michigan for mineral baths and treatments known as "electrical applications." For a time her health improved, but soon the neuritis recurred, and she developed an abdominal tumor. The presence of the tumor was confirmed by Dr. Leon J. Willien of Terre Haute in October of 1902, but the physician chose not to remove it.

While Sister Mary Theodosia was a student at the Academy, she met several of the Sisters of Providence who had ministered with Mother Theodore—Sisters Basilide, Mary Joseph, Olympiade, Mary Xavier, Mother Mary Cecilia and others. Given as she was to writing, she spent long hours with these sisters, carefully listening and recording their memories of Mother Theodore and the early years of the Congregation.

In 1900, when Bishop Chatard asked Mother Mary Cleophas Foley, superior general at the time, to assign a sister to write a book about Mother Theodore's life and spirituality, she turned to Sister Mary Theodosia. Sister Mary Theodosia accepted the task, and the book, "The Life and Life-Work of Mother Theodore Guerin—Foundress of the Sisters of Providence of Saint Mary-of-the-Woods, Indiana," was published in 1904. The work was an act of love and devotion. Because of the pain caused by the neuritis, Sister Mary Theodosia could not lift her right arm. She wrote the manuscript in lead pencil with the paper resting at knee height.

In October of 1906, Sister Mary Theodosia discovered a tumor in her left breast and immediately consulted Dr. Willien, who diagnosed the tumor as a severe malignancy. The physician advised immediate surgery. Without surgery, he said, she would not live longer than a month. The tumor was removed November 2, 1906, during a mastectomy at a hospital in Terre Haute. Fearing that Sister Mary Theodosia would not survive additional surgery, Dr. Willien did not disturb the abdominal tumor. The mastectomy damaged the nerves and muscles of Sister Mary Theodosia's left side, leaving her left arm rigid at her side.

Still, the cancer persisted. Only three months after the surgery, Dr. Willien determined that the malignancy was spreading; at the same time, the abdominal tumor was growing. Sister Mary Theodosia's condition deteriorated rapidly. Historical documents state: "... Sister Mary Theodosia suffered from dizziness and fainting. She had almost continuous vomiting. The abdominal tumor became so large that she was obliged to take her meals standing. ... She was no longer able to kneel, and she walked with difficulty." Sister Mary Theodosia, who was forty-eight years old, continued writing and editing articles, poems and stories.

On the evening of October 30, 1908, Sister Mary Theodosia paused at Mother Theodore's tomb to pray. She did not pray for herself, but for Sister Joseph Therese O'Connell who was very ill.

Sister Mary Theodosia recorded the events that followed in a letter to Mother Mary Cleophas. The letter, dated November 21, 1908, follows:

"I feel so happy, yet so abashed, over my cure, the story of which I shall now try to relate. Why should I be favored above the many who have so fervently sought cures through the intercession of our beloved and holy foundress?

"Friday evening, October 30, 1908, I visited the vault where repose the remains of our holy foundress, Mother Theodore. It was no special purpose that took me there; I was only passing up from the crypt chapel and stopped to say my customary prayers there—the *De Profundis, Gloria Patri*, the *Memorare*, and once 'Glory O Mary forever!' Mother Theodore's oft-repeated exclamation in her diary.

"While standing there, the thought came into my mind, 'I wonder if she has any power with Almighty God.'

Instantly I heard in my soul the words, 'Yes, she has.'

"I was so startled by the suddenness and distinctness of the words—not any external voice or sound, but an utterance to my soul—that I hurried away from the vault, fearing that in another moment I might perhaps see something.

"At the head of the stairs, I paused and reproached myself for my excitement, or rather a feeling of opposition—I did not want to see or hear anything—it was scarcely excitement. I am never afraid of the dead; why should I fear now?

"The words, 'Yes, she has,' came back to my mind, and then I said to myself, 'Well if she has, I wish she would show it.' My wish did not mean in regard to myself. I was hoping for Sister Joseph Therese's cure. With this I dismissed the subject from my mind and went to my room to work. It was then about half-past seven. I had been to confession and had remained to make the Way of the Cross when everybody was gone, standing at each station, as I was no longer able to genuflect or kneel.

"As my mind was greatly occupied that night with heavy proofreading and preparing another article for the printers, my little experience at the vault did not disturb me. I worked rapidly, unconscious of the hour till all was finished, a quarter to one o'clock. Then I hurried to bed and soon fell asleep.

"In the morning when I arose, I felt thoroughly rested and strong, although I had been in bed only a little over three hours. Without adverting to the fact for some moments, I spread my coverlet with both arms; hitherto I could use only my right arm and it was always a long and painful effort to get my bed made. My left arm was now perfectly good again. Then, for the first time in twenty months, I could roll up my hair without resting my head on my knees. My fingers are now as strong and quick on the typewriter, piano, etc., as if I had kept in daily practice.

"In dressing, I found that the bands of my clothing had to be lapped over about four inches. The enlargement at the waist had disappeared, and the weight that prevented me from genuflecting was no longer felt. What became of the lump, I do not know; but I feel nothing abnormal since that day.

"Moreover, I can see now as I never saw before. You know how poor my sight has always been. ... It is truly wonderful. But what seems to me the most wonderful of all is my perfect digestion. I can now eat anything that comes to the table, and in such quantities as to amaze everyone, considering that, for about twenty-four years, I had been the worst kind of a dyspeptic, dieting always and for long periods able to take no solid food whatever, and, of course, suffering much from the condition. It is truly most wonderful. Blessed be God in his saints. To Mother Theodore I owe all this.

"The vigor of my appearance now, the celerity of my movements and strength of voice—all are noted by the sisters, who often ask me what has happened. To one and all I have only this to say—Mother Theodore cured me.

"Three weeks ago tonight it happened, and I have not had a sick hour since. From the time I began writing the life of our holy foundress, I have felt like praying to her; but I never asked to be cured, except at the time when her remains were transferred to the crypt; when, at your bidding, dear Mother, I prayed, rather half-heartedly though, as I had no desire to live. For spiritual and even temporal favors, my petitions have been frequent and earnest, and nearly always answered.

"Dear Mother, I beg of you to thank God for the goodness to me, and to add to this what you see and know of my cure—to the praise and glory of our beloved and holy foundress, dear Mother Theodore."

In the months and years that followed, Sister Mary Theodosia was examined at various medical facilities in the United States. No trace of malignancy ever again was found. She died of heart disease March 23, 1943, at the age of eighty-two years, eight months and seven days—thirty-four years after the cure.

11

The Beatification of Mother Theodore Guerin

What have we to do in order to be saints? Nothing extraordinary; nothing more than what we do every day. Only do it for his love.

Mother Theodore Guerin

On the glorious morning of Sunday, October 25, 1998, a breezy patchwork day of sunshine and clouds, Sisters of Providence, friends and companions gathered in St. Peter's Square at Vatican City for the beatification of Mother Theodore Guerin. On this day, Mother Theodore, foundress of the Sisters of Providence; Rev. Faustino Miguez of Spain, founder of the Daughters of the Divine Shepherd; Don Zefirino Agostini of Italy, founder of the Ursuline Daughters of Mary Immaculate; and Rev. Antonio de Sant'Ana Galvao, OFM, of Brazil, were named blessed.

Several thousand pilgrims (people on a sacred journey) chanted and sang in Portuguese, Italian, French, Spanish and English while awaiting the opening of the ceremony and the presence of Pope John Paul II. Pilgrims honoring Mother Theodore wore silky blue scarves imprinted with her likeness. Soft brown cloth covered four tapestry portraits displayed on the facade of St. Peter's Basilica. Occasionally, the breeze lifted the cloth covering the portrait of Mother Theodore, and the pilgrims cheered.

Suddenly, in late morning, the crowd was hushed—save for the song of the wind—as Pope John Paul II stepped from the basilica to begin the beatification ceremony. The Pope honored Mother Theodore with powerful words: "Mother Theodore Guerin, foundress of the Sisters of Providence of Saint Mary-of-the-Woods, Indiana, holy woman of God, lived a life of extraordinary love. Her love for God totally filled her being. From that love came her deep caring for people in their sufferings and in their joys. Her love embraced even those who caused her pain and anguish. She transformed the hardest hearts by her inspired words.

Mother Theodore was truly a humble woman of God. While she possessed all the gifts necessary for leadership and used them brilliantly, she was always humble and gave God credit for all the good she did.

Her trust in her provident God was ever present in her life. In founding the Sisters of Providence of Saint Mary-of-the-Woods, Indiana, she called upon God's Providence in all things. In her words, 'Put yourself gently into the hands of Providence,' she recognized that all she did was in God's loving care. In the midst of trials and suffering, she embraced her crosses with full confidence that God would provide. She refused God no sacrifice that was asked of her.

Her life was a perfect blend of humanness and holiness. She was fully human, fully alive, yet her deep spirituality was woven visibly through the very fabric of her life. The woman, Mother Theodore Guerin, is indeed a woman for our time. She is a model of the best of womanhood. We present her to the world this day as blessed."

The long-awaited ceremony proclaimed to the entire world what Sisters of Providence and their friends have long known: that Mother Theodore Guerin, now Blessed Mother Theodore Guerin, is a holy woman in heaven with the God whom she served, loved and proclaimed throughout her life.

Four bishops from Indiana—Archbishop Daniel M. Beuchlein, OSB, of the Archdiocese of Indianapolis, Bishop Gerald Gettelfinger of the Diocese of Evansville, Bishop Dale Melczek of the Diocese of Gary, and Bishop William Higi of the Diocese of Lafayette-in-Indiana — concelebrated the Eucharistic Liturgy with Pope John Paul II.

Archbishop Beuchlein said, "Mother Theodore's beatification sends a clear message to citizens of Indiana and the United States that holy people really do exist. We have in Mother Theodore a true pioneer who left her native land of France and journeyed into the wilderness of Indiana. ... I am struck by her ability to keep her feet firmly planted on the ground while still being a very spiritual person. I believe that is a mark of true spirituality."

A Gift for the Pope Changes Lives

During the ceremony, the Sisters of Providence Congregation presented a gift and a reliquary (display case) containing a relic to Pope John Paul II. A relic is something sacred related to the holy person. In this instance, the relic was a piece of bone.

The gift was a wooden plaque carved from a tree at Saint Mary-of-the-Woods. The inscription on the plaque opens with these words: "On the occasion of the beatification of Mother

Theodore Guerin, our foundress, we, the Sisters of Providence of Saint Mary-of-the-Woods, Indiana, recall the generosity of the pioneer family of Saint Mary-of-the-Woods who offered housing to Mother Theodore and her five companions when they reached the dense forest of Indiana in 1840 only to find themselves homeless. It is fitting that we, her daughters, respond now to the housing needs of our neighbors in West Terre Haute, Indiana, by establishing a revolving loan fund of $50,000 which will help to make adequate housing available to those who could not otherwise afford it.

"We present this gift in the name of Pope John Paul II, whose words challenge us: 'The poor of the United States and of the world are your brothers and sisters in Christ. You must never be content to leave them just the crumbs of the feast. You must treat them like guests at your family table.' … May this gift of Providence help to build a community of love, mercy and justice."

People from many lands made the pilgrimage to the Vatican for the beatification of Mother Theodore. Among the many friends sharing the long-awaited celebration with the Sisters of Providence were Sisters of Providence of Ruillé-sur-Loir, France (the congregation of women religious who sent Mother Theodore to establish the mission at Saint Mary-of-the-Woods); Abbé Alfred Levitoux, pastor of St. John the Baptist Church at Etables (Mother Theodore's childhood parish); descendants of the Guérin family and the Thralls family (the farm family that provided refuge for Mother Theodore and her companions when they first arrived at Saint Mary-of-the-Woods); and representatives of the family of Sister Mary Theodosia Mug, who was cured of cancer after praying for Mother Theodore's intercession on behalf of another Sister of Providence.

For those who made the sacred journey to Rome, the beatification celebrations began with a prayer vigil late Saturday afternoon at St. Ignatius Church and concluded with a Mass of Thanksgiving on Monday morning at the Basilica of St. Paul Outside the Walls.

Likewise, Sisters of Providence remaining at Saint Mary-of-the-Woods were joined by friends and relatives to celebrate the beatification with a prayer vigil, a special Eucharistic Liturgy and a Mass of Thanksgiving. The celebrations mirrored as closely as possible those at the Vatican.

Thus, the Cause for Mother Theodore Guerin, opened in 1909, entered a new era. Now, in addition to honoring Mother Theodore as Blessed, the Congregation she established in 1840 began awaiting the second miracle that would enable her to be proclaimed a saint.

12

Honoring Blessed Mother Theodore Guerin

What does it matter what becomes of us, provided God's work be accomplished?
—Mother Theodore Guerin

After the beatification of Mother Theodore Guerin, Sister Diane Ris, general superior of the Sisters of Providence Congregation at the time, said quietly, "Now Mother Theodore belongs to the world." In the days, months and years that followed, the wisdom of Sister Diane's words was realized in countless tributes, honors, prayer requests and testimonies of devotion to Blessed Mother Theodore.

In February of 1999, the people of Indiana celebrated the beatification during a special Eucharistic Liturgy in the Church of the Immaculate Conception at Saint Mary-of-the-Woods. More than 600 people from across the state listened intently as Archbishop Buechlein of the Archdiocese of Indianapolis noted,

"This Eucharistic celebration is a historic first for Indiana. Few church provinces in our country have the joy and privilege to claim a beatified intercessor as one of their own."

The Archbishop said Blessed Mother Theodore is an "apt intercessor and a spiritual friend … on our journey of hope." He spoke of Mother Theodore as a model of authenticity, spiritual courage, devout prayer, balance of everyday life, zeal for missionary evangelization and patience in sickness. Archbishop Buechlein said, "In a word, all of us can find a friend and intercessor in our new and special patroness. Let's share this gift with our sisters and brothers in faith. Let's make her story our story."

And so, the story of Mother Theodore Guerin began anew, on the eve of the new millennium.

A gift that serves

As already mentioned, during the beatification ceremony the Sisters of Providence—in honor of Mother Theodore—presented to Pope John Paul II a plaque and a monetary gift designated for affordable housing. The inscription on the plaque opens with words spoken on another occasion by the Pope: *We must break open the cycles of despair in which are imprisoned all those who lack decent food, shelter or employment...*

A few months later, Pope John Paul II returned the gift to the Sisters of Providence. In a brief letter the Vatican's Secretary of State wrote: "His Holiness has now directed me to return the money to your Congregation for the establishment of a revolving loan fund aimed at building homes for the poor. It is his hope that this worthy initiative, which eloquently reflects Mother Guerin's witness of evangelical concern for those in need, will assist individuals and families in their efforts to secure a more humane standard of living."

The Sisters of Providence elected to use the gift as seed money to establish Providence Housing Corporation, a not-for-profit corporation providing affordable housing rehabilitation and community organization in the town of West Terre Haute, Indiana. From the start of rehabilitation of the first home in August 2000 through April of 2006, the corporation rehabilitated and/or repaired thirty-three homes belonging to low-income and/or elderly individuals and families.

With the gift, the corporation purchased twenty acres for the development of an affordable housing project named Providence Place. By May 2006, the corporation had constructed—at Providence Place—thirty-three two-bedroom apartments for senior citizens with limited income; eight single-family homes for first-time homeowners with limited income; and an office facility with a gathering place.

With the gift as seed money, by May 2006, Providence Housing Corporation had generated more than $3 million for housing rehabilitation, repairs and new construction, truly beginning to change the face of the community of West Terre Haute.

Also in 1999, in keeping with Mother Theodore's legacy of caring for those in need, Providence Self Sufficiency Ministries, a sponsored, incorporated ministry of the Sisters of Providence, began an expansion project that continues to evolve and grow. Providence Self Sufficiency Ministries was established in August 1994 in New Albany, Indiana, and opened Providence House for Children at the same time. Providence House provides care and shelter for abused and neglected children.

In 1999, the Archdiocese of Indianapolis gifted Providence Self Sufficiency Ministries with twelve acres of land in the community of Georgetown, Indiana. A separate corporation, Guerin Inc., named in honor of Mother Theodore, was formed to build facilities on the land.

The Providence House for Children campus has grown to include two group homes for girls and boys referred by the courts and six furnished apartments for families reuniting with children in foster care or families in danger of separation because they are homeless or live in substandard housing. One of the apartment dwellings for families is known as Guerin House and is dedicated to Mother Theodore.

In 2005, Guerin Inc. opened Guerin Woods, a development for senior citizens that adjoins the Providence House campus. On the Guerin Woods site are apartments for senior citizens with limited incomes and a senior citizens center. Guerin Woods honors Mother Theodore and "the Woods," the endearing expression Sisters of Providence use to refer to Saint Mary-of-the-Woods.

At Saint Mary of the Woods

In June 2003 the Sisters of Providence blessed and dedicated Mother Theodore Hall, a newly constructed health care facility with a physical and occupational therapy wing and a wing specially designed for residents with dementia.

A portrait of Mother Theodore is prominently displayed in Mother Theodore Hall, along with a copy of a letter she sent to Sisters of Providence ministering in Madison, Indiana, during a cholera outbreak. In the letter, dated March 2, 1849, Mother Theodore wrote, "… arm yourselves with courage and devote yourselves generously to the care of your suffering brethren. Without distinction of persons do good to all for the love of God, and if you have to die, die for Him who died for you." Stained-glass windows in the Mother Theodore Hall chapel cast sparkling rainbows of light on Sisters of Providence as they gather to pray.

Elsewhere on the motherhouse grounds, working in a quiet, towering, open space in the water treatment plant, artist/sculptor Teresa Clark created a six-foot-tall statue of Mother Theodore to be carved from Indiana limestone and displayed in Mary's Garden behind the Basilica of the National Shrine of the Immaculate Conception in Washington, D.C. The likeness reflects Mother Theodore's compassionate, loving spirit and innate grace and gives pause to all who view it. Dedicated to faithful women, the garden celebrates Mary, the mother of Jesus, as a model of faithful and committed living. Members of the National Council of Catholic Women are benefactors of the garden.

In Indiana and elsewhere

In May of 2000, Bishop Higi of the Diocese of Lafayette-in-Indiana recalled the beatification ceremony: "During the October 1998 beatification ceremony at the Vatican, I prayerfully asked Mother Theodore to intercede on behalf of my brother priests and myself that, like her, we might be consumed with love for the Church we have been called to serve, and for the people to whom we have been commissioned to minister, and to do that with unreserved hearts. … Her impact here in the State of Indiana, especially, but beyond our borders as well, was remarkable."

A few weeks later, Bishop Higi announced that the diocese would construct a new high school in Noblesville, near Indianapolis. Blessed Theodore Guerin High School opened in the fall of 2004, the first new Catholic high school built in the state of Indiana in thirty years. Each year the freshman class accompanied by the school's chaplain, school administrators and faculty members celebrate a day of heritage by making a pilgrimage to Saint Mary-of-the-Woods to pray and visit Mother Theodore's shrine.

Bishop John D'Arcy of the Diocese of Fort Wayne-South Bend announced that a new mausoleum garden crypt in a Catholic cemetery in Fort Wayne would be named in honor of

Mother Theodore. Blessed Mother Theodore Guerin Mausoleum was dedicated May 14, 2001, the 145th anniversary of her death.

In Indianapolis, Saint Joan of Arc Elementary School administrators established a scholarship fund in honor of Mother Theodore ensuring that recognition of her devotion to providing quality education endures.

And in March 2001, the House of Representatives of the Indiana General Assembly passed a resolution urging the Department of Transportation to name a portion of U.S. Highway 150, the road leading from West Terre Haute to Saint Mary-of-the-Woods, in honor of Mother Theodore.

In the summer of 2002, a tapestry portrait of Mother Theodore was placed in the hallway of a new perpetual adoration chapel at Our Lady of Mount Carmel Church in Carmel, Indiana. In October 2003, the Diocese of Fort Wayne-South Bend presented the first annual Blessed Mother Theodore Award to a director of religious education. The award is given to those who exemplify the qualities modeled by Mother Theodore.

In April of 2004, Saint John Bosco Parish in Churubusco, Indiana, in the Fort Wayne-South Bend Diocese, dedicated a newly renovated and enlarged catechetical center in honor of Mother Theodore. The following September, Saint John Parish in Indianapolis dedicated a shrine in the church honoring Mother Theodore. Saint John is the oldest parish in Indianapolis, and Sisters of Providence ministered at Saint John Academy from 1859 to 1959.

During Holy Week in 2006, Saint Roch Catholic Church in Indianapolis installed a large stained glass window of Blessed Mother Theodore.

Using a photograph on the Blessed Mother Theodore Guerin prayer card as a model, an artist carved a bust of Mother

Theodore to be displayed in the chapel of Fort McCoy Army Post, Fort McCoy, Wisconsin. The bust was created at the request of Msgr. Matthew G. Molner.

A watercolor portrait of Mother Theodore was shipped to the Office of the Cause at Saint Mary-of-the-Woods from LaPaz, Bolivia. A simple prayer asking Blessed Mother Theodore to "lighten our illnesses of body and soul" accompanied the painting.

The year 2002 was a time of tribute for the people of Etables-sur-Mer, France, where parishioners led by Abbé Alfred Levitoux, pastor of Saint Jean-Baptiste Church, restored Mother Theodore's birthplace home. A sign in the French language proclaims the reverence the people of the village have for Mother Theodore: *Maison Natale d'Anne Thérèse Guérin (1798–1856). Bienheureuse Mere Theodore, Fondatrice de la Congregation de la Providence de Ste Marie des Bois (Indiana).*

Mother Theodore's Feast Day

Holy people recognized by the Catholic Church are given special days of honor known as feast days. The Vatican has designated October 3 as Mother Theodore's feast day. October is a special month in Mother Theodore's life. She was born October 2, 1798, and was baptized Anne-Thérèse Guérin soon after birth. She arrived at Saint Mary-of-the-Woods the evening of October 22, 1840. She received the title "Blessed" on October 25, 1998, and was canonized on October 15, 2006.

The first celebration of Mother Theodore's feast day was October 3, 1999. At Saint Mary-of-the-Woods, Sisters of Providence celebrate the feast day with a Eucharistic Liturgy and special veneration of Mother Theodore's shrine in the Church of the Immaculate Conception. Feast day remembrance services honoring Mother Theodore are celebrated across the United States, Taiwan, France, England and other lands.

The collect or prayer for Mother Theodore's feast is a reminder of her holiness: "Loving God, in Saint Mother Theodore Guerin you have given us an example of a religious woman who trusted deeply in Providence. Through her intercession, inspire us to dedicate our lives to proclaiming the gospel through works of love, mercy and justice." The prayer is used during the Eucharistic Liturgy.

In their own time and in their own ways, people across the United States celebrate Mother Theodore.

Sisters of Providence have ministered in the Archdiocese of Boston for decades. Cardinal Bernard Law presided during a celebration honoring Mother Theodore at Saint Rose Church in Chelsea, Massachusetts. Sister Mary Theodosia Mug, whose cure through the intercession of Mother Theodore was approved as a miracle, was one of fifteen Sisters of Providence who opened the mission at Saint Rose in 1889.

Speaking at Marywood Retreat Center in Orange, California, Sister Marie Kevin Tighe, vice postulator of the Cause for Mother Theodore, urged those attending to consider developing a lifetime friendship with Mother Theodore, a woman of faith and courage, as a model for Christian lives, gospel living and gospel loving. "Turn to her in your time of need, asking her to intercede for us with God," Sister Marie Kevin said. "She then becomes our intercessor, presenting our concerns, cares and needs to God on our behalf. ... We believe in the Communion of Saints, that is, that all of us who are still on Earth are bonded with those who have gone before us. We believe that they are aware of us and are ready to be our special intercessors before the throne of God."

Sister Marie Kevin added, "Mother Theodore was alive and aware. She was loving and affectionate, willing to take the risk of challenging her friends. She was a woman of the world, a woman of deep prayer. She held all persons in great reverence."

Sister Marie Kevin asked each person to consider this thought: "How is Mother Theodore a model for me in this place and time?"

People given to the written word were inspired to include Mother Theodore in numerous publications, newspapers, books and personal columns. Some examples follow.

Writing in the "Bishop's Forum," a column in the newspaper of the Evansville Diocese, Bishop Gerald Gettelfinger said, "She is our local saint. 'Blessed' she is but 'Saint' to us. She is already at work for us before the throne of God."

The fourth revised edition of "Saint of the Day: Lives, Lessons and Feasts" contains a segment about Mother Theodore. She is included as an inspiration in "Saints from A to Z: An Inspirational Dictionary" written by Cindy Cavnar. An article about Mother Theodore is featured in the 2007 edition of the Harcourt Religion Series for Grade 7. Nelson Price wrote about Mother Theodore in "Legendary Hoosiers," a book for children and young adults. The Los Angeles Tidings newspaper featured an article titled, "The Power of Saints—Heavenly Prayers to Cure Earthly Illnesses," about the miracle cure of Sister Mary Theodosia Mug. Books, prayer booklets and prayer cards have been translated into numerous languages enabling people of many lands to know Mother Theodore as a spiritual companion and inspiration.

13

Praying with Blessed Mother Theodore Guerin

Try then, today, to deliver into the hands of our sweet Jesus all the care of the future, as well as all anxiety about the past.

—Mother Theodore Guerin

"I saw a picture of Mother Theodore and I felt drawn to her."

With these few words one individual writing to the Office for the Promotion of the Cause of Mother Theodore Guerin expressed what so many of the world's people have experienced. Requests for prayers and reports of favors granted through the intercession of Mother Theodore have been evident for decades, even before the opening of the Cause in 1909. In recent years, however, as Mother Theodore's life, legacy and holiness became more widely known, the reports of prayers offered through her intercession are more frequent. Prayer sustained Mother

Theodore through the joys and sorrows of her life. Now, people of all ages and nationalities find comfort in Mother Theodore, a holy woman for all time.

Tender ... poignant ... desperate ... forlorn ... hopeful ... grateful...

The letters mirror the lives of countless individuals and families, and illustrate the strength that is born of faith — and prayer.

Finding hope in prayer

A family in France tells of a daughter who was hospitalized because of rapid, uncontrolled weight loss and anorexia. The family prayed for the intercession of Mother Theodore and the girl now is taking meals with her family.

In 1989, a Franciscan Sister of Oldenburg, Indiana, gave a relic of Mother Theodore to a young girl with a malignant brain tumor. The girl's family fastened the relic around her ankle the evening before her second surgery; no malignant cells were found. The physicians said the child would never walk again, but from their home in Waldron, Indiana, the family writes that she walks, runs and jumps.

In a letter, a young man from St. Paul, Minnesota, said he kept a drawing of Mother Theodore on his refrigerator. He said he was praying through Mother Theodore's intercession for people suffering from alcoholism and, also, for help as he prepared for exams for a pastoral ministry degree in liturgy. "I just felt drawn to the picture with the trees behind her," he wrote.

A woman in Indianapolis wrote that the day after Thanksgiving, her son, a doctor, fell from a ladder and crushed his head on a cement porch. He was in a coma four weeks. "I put his recovery in the hands of Blessed Mother Theodore

Guerin," the woman said. Her son opened his eyes on Christmas Eve.

From France, a woman wrote that her seven-year-old grandson, Etienne, survived a horrendous car crash that killed his mother. Though the child was in a coma, the family placed a prayer card of Mother Theodore on his pillow. He awoke from the coma and recovered.

A physician, the father of three children, said his daughter with aplastic anemia is in remission. He said the family is convinced that the child's improving condition is the result of answered prayers, "especially answered prayers through the intercession of Mother Theodore Guerin."

One request for prayers was from the family of a thirty-five-year-old mother of three children who was suffering from "widespread" cancer. The woman is from Indiana. Another was for a nine-year-old girl in New Jersey with a rare neurological disorder. And another was for a fifty-one-year-old woman in South Carolina preparing for brain surgery and an experimental treatment.

Generations of devotion

In 2000, a man shared the stories of three generations of devotion to Mother Theodore. He asked the Sisters of Providence to join the family in praying for Mother Theodore's intercession for a member of the third generation, his son living in Florida, who was to undergo surgery and radiation for brain cancer. The first generation story involved the father of three children who was out of work five months when he offered a novena (nine days of prayer) to Mother Theodore and soon received a telegram from his former company informing him that work was available. A son, a member of the second generation, was diagnosed with Guillain-Barré Syndrome, a rare neurological disorder. He was given a relic and a prayer card of Mother Theodore, and his condition improved.

That the human condition is fragile and fraught with unbelievable suffering is evident in the letters mailed to the Office of the Promotion of the Cause on behalf of Mother Theodore.

Requests for prayers in early 2001 were for, among others, a five-year-old girl with dislocated hips; a three-year-old boy with cerebral palsy; a six-year-old girl with leukemia; and a young mother with lung cancer. The aunt of a nineteen-year-old girl with multiple problems including substance abuse wrote: "Mother Theodore devoted her life to children, first to her siblings and then to all of God's children. With Mother Theodore's intercession on behalf of my niece, we are joining with her on this seemingly long haul."

In gratitude

A letter from a Sister of Providence in France was filled with gratitude. The woman was orphaned at age two and raised in an orphanage at Ruillé-sur-Loir. As an adult, she entered the Sisters of Providence there. In 1997, she suffered a pulmonary embolism with complications and was in a coma several weeks. Sisters in the congregation wrote to Saint Mary-of-the-Woods asking for prayers through the intercession of Mother Theodore. Later, the sister wrote: "I am really well. The specialist calls me a miracle. Please let us thank Meré Theodore and thank you again for your prayers. I was under oxygen for two years and now I don't need it anymore, although when I left the hospital the doctor said to me, 'Sister, you may need oxygen all of your life.' "

In 2002, a priest shared these events: "Ten days ago, my right hand was suddenly paralyzed so that I couldn't elevate the chalice during Mass or click the mouse on my computer. After two days of suffering, I had a long friendly talk with Mother Theodore and said one Hail Mary. On the same evening, I felt an atrocious pain in the whole hand for a moment and then after that the forces gradually returned to my arm so that I am able to use it again."

In 2003, a teacher at a Catholic school in Pennsylvania, a graduate of Mother Theodore Guerin High School in River Grove, Illinois, shared a personal story. While teaching an eighth-grade class about the history of the Catholic Church she asked the students to research the life of Blessed Mother Theodore. Some time later, a boy in the first grade was diagnosed with bacterial meningitis. "His prognosis was grim," the teacher wrote. "I entrusted his life to Blessed Mother Theodore's intercession. He survived and went home. I am confident that Mother Guerin's intercession played a critical part in his recovery."

The Office for the Promotion of the Cause at Saint Mary-of-the-Woods has received letters with reports of favors granted and requests for prayers, relics and information from countries such as Sri Lanka, Argentina, Belgium, Poland, Germany, England, Ireland, Italy, the Netherlands, Canada, Saudi Arabia, Thailand, Bolivia, Mexico and France. The writer of a letter from Spain asked for pictures and leaflets and added, "We like the example of Mother Theodore's life."

These are but a sampling of the thousands of requests for assistance and guidance through the intercession of Mother Theodore that have been recorded. Other individuals and families find solace and strength during pilgrimages to Saint Mary-of-the-Woods, where they visit her shrine to seek health, well being, recovery and peace for loved ones through the intercession of Mother Theodore.

14

The Second Miracle

You will see many things in new light if you give the Holy Spirit free access to your minds and your hearts.
—Mother Theodore Guerin

The fabric of Mother Theodore's life was woven with prayer. Prayer was her sustenance, giving her inspiration, strength, hope and assurance. During those first years in Indiana, when the Sisters of Providence were struggling to survive, no strangers to hunger, loneliness, poverty, prejudice, extreme weather and illness, Mother Theodore compassionately and consistently encouraged them to pray.

This legacy of prayer has continued through the years wherever Sisters of Providence live and minister. Sisters of Providence gather in the Church of the Immaculate Conception, the Blessed Sacrament Chapel, the chapel in Mother Theodore Hall and at many other locations at Saint Mary-of-the-Woods for prayer and worship. They pause at the shrine honoring Mary as Our Lady of Providence and at Mother Theodore's shrine and stroll through the Sisters of Providence Cemetery for quiet moments of reflection and meditation.

And so it was in this special place, this wooded, ravine-cut ground where Mother Theodore once walked, that the second miracle occurred, the miracle that cleared the way for the canonization of Mother Theodore. Like the healing of Sister Mary Theodosia Mug in 1908, this most recent miracle began with a simple prayer seeking strength and assistance through the intercession of Mother Theodore.

'I said a prayer'

Phil McCord, whose sight was restored, considers himself to be an unlikely candidate for a miracle. His affiliation with the Sisters of Providence began in 1997 when he was hired to serve as Director of Facilities Management. In his words, "I oversee the physical component of the motherhouse, everything from mowing the grass to building maintenance to security." Phil was born May 23, 1946, and grew up in Anderson, Indiana. He and his wife are the parents of three adult children. Before accepting the position with the Sisters of Providence he worked as director of engineering for two large hospitals. "I didn't know the Sisters of Providence before beginning the job here," he said. "I am not Catholic formally."

Phil's journey to the miracle began in May of 1998 when an eye examination revealed that he was developing cataracts. Over the next several months, his sight declined, and in December he was fitted with new eyeglasses. Finally, he decided to have the cataracts surgically removed. Surgery on his left eye was scheduled for September 21. The surgery was successful. In a matter of days, the vision in his left eye was 20–20.

In October, he went for surgery to remove the cataract on his right eye. He remembers: "Everything was the same: the same doctor, the same technician, the same operating room." Except, this time, there were complications: edema and inflammation. Phil treated the eye with prescribed medications, but the condition did not improve; the edema in the cornea was persistent. He was referred for treatment to an eye institute in Indianapolis, where the physician recommended a transplant of the cornea to save his sight. The procedure, the physician cautioned, was not without risk of side effects: hemorrhage in the eye, infection, rejection, blindness, death. He told Phil to think about the transplant as an option and then to return in a month to schedule the surgery.

Reflecting on those thirty days of indecision and fear, Phil remembers: "The doctor said the eye wouldn't heal itself, but the more I thought about the surgery the more squeamish I felt. I could only see light and shapes through the eye. It was like holding a tissue to your eye and looking through it. The eye drooped on one side, and it had an ache in it, a dull, low-level ache. It was annoying. Finally, I about convinced myself that I could not have the surgery."

The fragility of all of the things people tend to take for granted weighed on Phil's mind. On the morning of January 3, 2001, he was walking in the quiet corridors outside the Church of the Immaculate Conception at Saint Mary-of-the-Woods. "I went in and sat down to try to think with a clear head," Phil says. There, seated in a wooden pew, winter light streaming through the stained glass windows, Phil spoke with God and with Mother Theodore. "God, I try not to bother you with a lot of things, but I can't do this. I need some help," he prayed. "And, Mother Theodore, if you have influence with God I'd appreciate it if you would say something. Please help me get through this."

Thoughtfully, Phil recalls, "I sat there another four or five minutes. I felt better, so I thought my prayer was answered. 'I can get through this,' I said to myself. I felt peaceful, and that is what I was asking for."

Comforted by the feelings of acceptance and peace, Phil finished his day of work. "The next morning I got up and showered and shaved. I felt different. My eye wasn't as droopy and it didn't ache. Things seemed a little lighter."

On January 26, Phil returned to Indianapolis. He remembers: "The physician looked at my eyes, then at my chart. He said, 'It is better. You don't need a transplant. The swelling is gone. There is some tissue from the old cataract but we can break that up with a laser. ... What did you do?' "

Phil replied, "I said a prayer."

The laser surgery to remove accumulations of protein was performed in Terre Haute. By March, the edema in the cornea was nearly gone, and by May the cornea was clear. "The entire process was a miracle," Phil reflects.

One day shortly after, Phil was working at Saint Mary-of-the-Woods when a Sister of Providence who also had cataract surgery approached him and asked about his eyes and his sight. He shared his story with her, and she exclaimed, "That is a miracle!"

"Yes, I think so," he replied.

The process begins

Remembering, Phil adds, "The next thing I knew Sister Marie Kevin Tighe (vice postulator of Mother Theodore's Cause) contacted me and the process began. It was as simple as that."

Phil says it never occurred to him to pray for a miracle, and the magnitude of the healing puzzles him. "I asked myself,

'What have I done to deserve this?' Finally, I reconciled myself to it. The Sisters of Providence remind me that I am God's child and I do not have to do something spectacular to receive a miracle!"

While it is not a part of the miracle healing approved by Vatican officials, Phil believes he experienced yet another miracle. About a year after his vision was restored and his eye was healed, he was diagnosed with cardiomyopathy, and he was given a five-year life expectancy without a heart transplant.

He was placed on medication. "I started getting things in order," he says. "The medications made me feel bad for about five months, and then I began to feel strong and was walking again. But my prognosis did not change." In the months that followed, however, Phil's heart responded to the medications, and, in May of 2006, his heart was described as "normal."

"The doctors told me I can work and that I can expect a normal life span. They said, 'Keep those sisters praying for you!' " he says with a smile. "It is remarkable. I am twice blessed. It is so humbling … to be a small part of Mother Theodore receiving the recognition that she deserves. I am so grateful; really, really tickled."

The yellow-gold light of the late afternoon sun falls across Phil's desk. He is silent several thoughtful seconds. He lifts his eyes and says, "Mother Theodore is inspiring."

15

The Canonization of Blessed Mother Theodore Guerin

We register them in the roll call of the saints.
Their names will be remembered forever.
— Pope Benedict XVI

As the days of autumn 2006 unfurled in glorious colors, cool nights and misty days, the moment of the canonization of Blessed Mother Theodore Guerin drew near. It was a time of reverence, anticipation, exhilaration and thankfulness.

At this same time of year in 1840, Mother Theodore and her five companions — Sister St. Vincent, Sister Basilide, Sister St. Liguori, Sister Marie Xavier and Sister Olympiade — had ended their perilous journey across the sea and were winding their way by boat, coach and wagon to their new mission at Saint Mary-of-the-Woods. They had no idea that a beautiful wilderness would be their home or that the years would unfold in months of desolation and hardship, cherished triumphs and sweet grace. They knew only that they were following the call of God in their hearts and in their lives. They were about to build a marvelous heritage, a heritage beyond imagining.

In preparation for Mother Theodore's canonization, a quiet and solemn ceremony took place at Saint Mary-of-the-Woods on her feast day, October 3, 2006. Her remains, placed in a simple casket of hand-hewn walnut, were reverently carried into the Church of the Immaculate Conception and placed at a new interim shrine in a front alcove. "We just recognized a holy woman," said Sister Denise Wilkinson, general superior of the Sisters of Providence. Sister Denise asked all present to "help one another be saints." At the conclusion of the ceremony, the large assembly quietly filed to the shrine one-by-one to venerate Mother Theodore and offer prayer.

Tony Dubois, woodworker and Facilities Management staff member at Saint Mary-of-the-Woods, was charged with the task of turning rough boards of walnut from a tree harvested on the grounds more than fifty years ago into the coffin which was to hold the precious remains of the foundress.

For several weeks Tony and his partner, Tim Wilson, also a staff member, were hard at work fashioning the coffin — measuring, cutting, sanding and filling in the imperfections in the wood. They fitted the coffin with "dovetail" joints and "floated the bottom" of the coffin so that the finished product could withstand temperature and moisture changes. The final touch was to apply tung oil, a common wood finish used in fine woodworking to accentuate the color and grain of the wood.

Tony said of the project, "When I chose the walnut board from the grounds on which Mother Theodore's mission to the world began to unfold, I became conscious that after planed, joined and assembled, it would be transformed into a sacred artifact. This realization filled me with the sense of the holy."

A few days after the transfer of remains, writing in his "Seeking the Face of the Lord" column in the Archdiocese of Indianapolis newspaper, The Criterion, Archbishop Daniel M. Buechlein heralded the canonization. "It is an extraordinary privilege for our archdiocese to have a canonized saint who is buried here [at Saint Mary-of-the-Woods]," he wrote. "When all is said and done, Saint Theodora is a model of the centrality of prayer from which all mission flows."

The Canonization of Mother Theodore Guerin in Rome

Thousands of pilgrims from across the world assembled for the canonization ceremony and Eucharistic Liturgy Sunday, October 15, 2006, in Saint Peter's Square at the Vatican. Tapestry portraits of the four new saints — Mother Theodore Guerin, the first saint from Indiana and the eighth from the United States of America; Rafael Guizar Valencia, the first saint from Mexico; Filippo Smaldone, an Italian who established a school for the deaf; and Sister Rosa Venerini, an Italian who opened the first public school for girls in Italy — were displayed on the facade of the magnificent basilica. Pilgrims honoring Mother Theodore waved silken blue scarves, handmade by Sisters of Providence, and proudly wore two-inch diameter buttons bearing her image. The five bishops from Indiana were among the pilgrims honoring Mother Theodore, along with the bishop from the diocese in France where Mother Theodore was born.

Describing her as "a beautiful spiritual figure and a model of Christian life and strength who had infinite confidence in Divine Providence," Pope Benedict XVI canonized Mother Theodore Guerin, the last of the four holy persons to be honored.

Speaking of Mother Theodore, the Pope continued: "'Go and sell everything you own, and give the money to the poor … then come, follow me.' These words have inspired countless Christians throughout the history of the Church to follow Christ in a life of radical poverty, trusting in Divine Providence. Among these generous disciples of Christ was a young French woman, who responded unreservedly to the call of the Divine Teacher. Mother Theodore Guerin entered the Congregation of the Sisters of Providence in 1823, and she devoted herself to the work of teaching in schools. Then in 1839, she was asked by her superiors to travel to the United States to become the head of a new community in Indiana. After their long journey over land and sea, the group of six sisters arrived at Saint Mary-of-the-Woods. There they found a simple log cabin chapel in the heart of the forest. They knelt down before the Blessed Sacrament and gave thanks, asking God's guidance upon the new foundation.

"With great trust in Divine Providence, Mother Theodore overcame many challenges and persevered in the work that the Lord had called her to do. By the time of her death in 1856, the sisters were running schools and orphanages throughout the state of Indiana. In her own words, 'How much good has been accomplished by the Sisters of Saint Mary-of-the-Woods. How much more good they will be able to do if they remain faithful to their holy vocation.'"

At the conclusion of the canonization service, Pope Benedict said: "I am happy to greet all the English-speaking pilgrims present today, especially those who have come for the canonization of Mother Theodore Guerin, foundress of the Sisters of Providence of Saint Mary-of-the-Woods. The Church rejoices in the four new saints raised to the altars today. May their example inspire us and their prayers obtain for us guidance and courage."

During the canonization ceremony, Sister Nancy Nolan, Sister Diane Ris and Sister Ann Margaret O'Hara, former general superiors of the Sisters of Providence Congregation during important phases of the Cause for the Beatification and Canonization of Mother Theodore, placed a reliquary containing a relic of Mother Theodore in a place of honor near the altar.

The Congregation also presented gifts to Pope Benedict XVI. Sister Denise Wilkinson, Sister Marie Kevin Tighe, vice postulator of the Cause, and Phil McCord, whose restored eyesight was declared a miracle healing through the intercession of Mother Theodore, presented a monetary gift to Pope Benedict XVI for the education of women and children. They also noted that monetary gifts in his name were given to several Congregation ministries: Guerin College Preparatory High School, River Grove, Illinois; Providence Cristo Rey High School, Indianapolis; Saint Mary-of-the-Woods College and Woods Day Care/Pre-School, both at Saint Mary-of-the-Woods; Providence Family Services, Chicago; Educational/Family Services, West Terre Haute, and Providence in the Desert, Indio, California.

Sisters of Providence attending the events in Rome took two small black books, each titled "Book of Names," to the canonization ceremony. The small black books contained more than 3,000 handwritten names of people who were unable to attend the canonization in Rome but desired to be present in spirit.

In anticipation of the canonization, pilgrims honoring Mother Theodore participated in a prayer vigil on Saturday evening, October 14, at the Church of the Gesú in Rome. The service included Scripture passages, readings from the writings of Mother Theodore and a presentation of Mother Theodore's life told in three parts: her childhood in Etables, her life as a Sister of Providence in France, and her life as a missionary in Indiana. As part of the vigil, pilgrims created a temporary shrine honoring Mother Theodore. Artifacts of Mother Theodore's life — a stone from her birthplace-home in Etables, her rosary, her worn white cross, a letter from her journal, a medallion given to her by the French government for her work in education — were each placed at the shrine in a solemn ritual of procession.

Archbishop Buechlein celebrated the Eucharistic Liturgy at a Mass of Thanksgiving on Monday morning, October 16, at the Basilica of Saint Paul Outside the Walls. The other bishops of Indiana, the bishop from France and several other priests concelebrated.

The archbishop said: "We now have a local saint to spur us onto victory. We have our own saint who continually prays for the strength of her community. ... God so loved our little part of the world to bless us with a remarkable woman. Canonization is an awesome gift. Let's not take for granted what Mother Theodore did for us. God gave us Mother Theodore's life as an example."

Celebrations in Indiana

Sisters of Providence, along with many pilgrims and other visitors, assembled at Saint Mary-of-the-Woods and devoted the October 15 weekend to prayer and celebration. A vigil prayer service was held Saturday evening and a Eucharistic Liturgy honoring Mother Theodore's canonization in Rome took place Sunday morning. Throughout the days a steady stream of people prayed at her shrine, lovingly placing their hands on the coffin holding her remains, and listing their special needs in the book of prayer intentions.

On Sunday afternoon, the Indianapolis Archdiocesan Office for Youth and Young Adult Ministries hosted a pilgrimage to Saint Mary-of-the-Woods as a special and memorable way for young people to celebrate the canonization. Once they arrived at

Saint Mary-of-the-Woods, the youths walked the paths once walked by Mother Theodore, attended Liturgy in the Church of the Immaculate Conception, and paused for prayer at the interim shrine honoring Saint Mother Theodore Guerin.

For Sisters of Providence and many relatives, former students, ministry associates friends and neighbors, the celebration of the canonization continued the next weekend with tours of the grounds and a special Eucharistic Liturgy Sunday afternoon, October 22, the 166th anniversary of the founding of the Sisters of Providence Congregation at Saint Mary-of-the-Woods. Members from the Mother Theodore Guerin Chapter of Knights of Columbus in Terre Haute and from other councils around the state led the entrance procession and stood guard at shrine.

Sister Denise Wilkinson presented a special reflection about Mother Theodore. "Today, this Foundation Day, we add a new, rich and complex pattern to our history as a Congregation — the experience of the institutional church's official recognition of our foundress as a Saint of God.

"In the weeks leading up to last Sunday's liturgy of canonization in Rome and in the days following, media personnel asked me one question — with slight variations — over and over again. What does the canonization mean for the citizens of the Wabash Valley; for citizens of Indiana; for non-Catholics; for former students and friends of the Sisters of Providence; for members of the Congregation?"

Sister Denise invited all "to ponder these questions in whatever group they found themselves and to find ways to talk with one another not only about this remarkable woman, but about our own hopes and aspirations and deep-seated convictions about issues important to her...

"...And to all here today, to all of us drawn by the spirit and the legacy of Saint Mother Theodore Guerin, let's ponder this one last question together and frequently. Do we, all of us here, so love and honor Mother Theodore Guerin, Saint of God, and so love the God of Providence that we will promise one another — with all our hearts — to do all we can to help one another become saints?"

And so, even as it ends, it begins.

While the Cause that spanned nearly 100 years is finished, a new era of sharing the life and spirituality of Mother Theodore is just beginning. Even today, all these many decades later, she is *real*. People of all ages, of all nationalities and of all religions look at her life and teachings and discover unexpected hope and inspiration.

Mother Theodore Guerin — Saint of God, a gift to the world.

16

Beloved Land

What will heaven be if our poor Earth is at times so beautiful?

—Mother Theodore Guerin

Even though she once considered it a land of exile, Mother Theodore grew to love Indiana. She traveled the state by carriage, boat and horseback from the flat fields in the north to the rugged forested hills in the south. She marveled at the seasons, describing in her letters and journals the glittering ice diamonds of winter and the relentless, sweltering heat of summer. She found solace during long walks in the woods, thanking God for the beauty, and seeking assistance and guidance.

The lay of the land at Saint Mary-of-the-Woods is little changed since Mother Theodore walked it. The ravines, the giant trees, the grasses and the wildflowers are constant. Saint Mary-of-the-Woods was, for Mother Theodore, a beloved place.

Mother Theodore's interim shrine

One of the first tributes to Mother Theodore in recognition of the beatification was the creation of a shrine in her honor, located in the entrance to the Church of Immaculate Conception.

After her canonization October 15, 2006, an interim shrine was erected under the banner-portrait of Mother Theodore that was displayed in St. Peter's Square in Rome. The shrine is located in the left front alcove of the Church of the Immaculate Conception. Saint Mother Theodore Guerin's remains rest in a walnut coffin in a place of honor on a platform covered with the same blue silk material used for the canonization pilgrimage scarves. A small, wooden reliquary containing three bones from Mother Theodore's hand is displayed to the left of the coffin. Pilgrims and visitors are invited to record prayer requests in a book on a table near the shrine. The Decree of Canonization is displayed to the right of the coffin.

At the time of this writing, a permanent shrine to Saint Mother Theodore is under consideration.

The Church of the Immaculate Conception

Built between 1886 and 1907, the Italian Renaissance-style church is constructed of Indiana limestone with red marble walls, frescoes and stained-glass windows created at the Bavarian Art Institute in Munich, Germany. The high altar was removed when the church was renovated in 1986, and the marble used for the Main altar, the altar of repose, the major and minor ambo and the presider's chair. A sculpture of the risen Christ adorns the center wall of the sanctuary. The Church of the Immaculate Conception is located at the heart of the motherhouse grounds. Sisters, guests and visitors gather there at 11 a.m. each Sunday and at 11:30 a.m. Monday through Saturday for Eucharistic Liturgy.

Historical markers

Three boulders on the motherhouse grounds indicate the locations of important historical events in Mother Theodore's life.

The marker of arrival is behind the Grotto of Our Lady of Lourdes. The inscription on the plaque tells the story: *This tablet marks the place where Mother Theodore and her five companions—Sister St. Vincent Ferrer, Sister Basilide, Sister St. Liguori, Sister Marie Xavier and Sister Olympiade—first stepped upon the soil of Saint Mary-of-the-Woods, October 22, 1840.*

The second stone marker indicates the site of the first Mass at Saint Mary-of-the-Woods. This boulder is located near Providence Hall, a red-brick building constructed in 1890: *The first Mass at Saint Mary-of-the-Woods was offered on this spot by Bishop Bruté, the first bishop of Vincennes, January 6, 1837, in the log hut dwelling of Father Buteux, who was on that date installed here as pastor.*

The third stone, located along the road opposite the Grotto, indicates the location of the first convent. The marker reads: *Site of first Providence Convent, founded October 22, 1840, by Mother Theodore Guerin.* Originally, the convent was the farmhouse home of Sarah and Joseph Thralls. For about a month, the 10 members of the Thralls family shared their home with Mother Theodore, the five Sisters of Providence from France, and four American postulants.

The Dioramas

Created in 1940 to celebrate the centennial of the founding of the Sisters of Providence Congregation at Saint Mary-of-the-

Woods, the dioramas consist of three-dimensional scenes depicting the early history of the Sisters of Providence. Brief audio descriptions accompany the scenes. The dioramas are located in Providence Center.

Our Lady of Lourdes Grotto

The Grotto of Our Lady of Lourdes is the largest of the outdoor shrines at Saint Mary-of-the-Woods. Construction began November 11, 1918, as a gesture of thanksgiving for the end of World War I.

Blessed Sacrament Chapel

The Blessed Sacrament Chapel was consecrated in 1924 as a place of Exposition and continual prayer. Here, Sisters of Providence maintain vigil each day, praying for the needs of the world and for people who ask for their prayers.

National Shrine of Our Lady of Providence

The National Shrine of Our of Lady of Providence is a reflection of the devotion the Sisters of Providence have for Mary, the mother of Jesus. The focal point of the shrine is a painting of Our Lady of Providence, a reproduction of the masterpiece by Scipione Pulzoni, known as Gaetano. The painting has been venerated since 1664 in the Church of San Carlo ai Catinari in Rome. At the national shrine, Mary is honored under the title Our Lady of Providence, Queen of the Home. The shrine is located in Providence Center.

Outdoor Way of the Cross

The Outdoor Way of the Cross follows a sidewalk path through a grove of trees between Providence Hall and the Sisters of Providence Cemetery. The Outdoor Way of the Cross has been in place since 1938.

Cemetery of the Sisters of Providence

More than 1,800 Sisters of Providence rest in the cemetery, which was established in 1861. A memorial lists the names of Sisters of Providence who are buried in other locations. A small relic of Mother Theodore is buried in the cemetery. A Celtic cross above Mother Theodore's grave is etched with these words from the Song of Songs: *I sleep but my heart watches over this house which I have built.*

Beloved land

These are among the historical landmarks at Saint Mary-of-the-Woods that are part of the legacy of Mother Theodore, reflections of her devotion to the Eucharist, to Mary, the mother of Jesus, and to prayer. Visitors are welcome to make pilgrimages to Saint Mary-of-the-Woods to walk this holy ground, visit Mother Theodore's shrine and pray with the Sisters of Providence.

A Summary of Sources

Journals and Letters of Mother Theodore Guerin, Foundress of the Sisters of Providence of Saint Mary-of-the-Woods, Indiana; edited with notes by Sister Mary Theodosia Mug, SP; Sisters of Providence, Saint Mary-of-the-Woods, Indiana; 1937, 1942, 1978.

The History of the Sisters of Providence of Saint Mary-of-the-Woods; by Sister Mary Borromeo Brown, SP; Benziger Brothers Inc.; 1949.

Positio Super Virtutibus for the Beatification and Canonization of Mother Theodore Guerin; compiled by Sister Joseph Eleanor Ryan, SP; Rome; 1987.

The Founding Spirit, a newsletter compiled by Sister Marie Kevin Tighe, SP, of the Office for the Promotion of the Cause; Saint Mary-of-the-Woods, Indiana.

Acknowledgements

Many people contributed to the creation of this book.

Editorial Board for Mother Theodore Guerin, A Woman for Our Time, published in 1998: Sister Diane Ris, general superior of the Sisters of Providence, and editorial board members: Sister Rosemary Borntrager, general secretary for the Congregation; Sister Eileen Ann Kelley, archivist for the Congregation; Sister Pam Pauloski, associate director of communications for the Office of Congregational Advancement; Sister Joan Slobig, a general officer for the Congregation; Sister Marie Kevin Tighe, promoter of the Cause for the Beatification and Canonization of Mother Theodore Guerin; Sister Denise Wilkinson, director of the Office of Congregational Advancement; and Katrina D. Thielman, designer and photographer for the Office of Congregational Advancement.

Editorial Board for Mother Theodore Guerin – Saint of God, A Woman for All Time, published in 2006: Sister Rosemary Borntrager, general secretary; Sister Mary Ryan, archivist for the Congregation; Sister Marie Kevin Tighe, vice postulator and promoter of the Cause; Sister Ann Casper, executive director of the Office of Congregational Advancement; Connie McCammon, publication manager and special projects associate for the Office of Congregational Advancement; and Diane Weidenbenner, director of marketing and communications of the Office of Congregational Advancement.

A number of people devoted years to collecting and documenting volumes of information for the Cause. The value of their work truly is beyond measure.

- There simply are no words to describe the tireless devotion Sister Marie Kevin Tighe gave to the Cause, first as promoter and then as vice postulator. She traveled to the Vatican countless times, answered letters and phone calls from people around the world seeking information about Mother Theodore and reporting favors granted through the intercession of Mother Theodore, and compiled The Founding Spirit newsletter.

- Sister Joseph Eleanor Ryan compiled the **Positio**, a huge document filled with letters and journals written by Mother Theodore, letters written to Mother Theodore, and memories and testimony of Sisters of Providence and others who knew Mother Theodore. The **Positio** truly is a treasure.

- Sister Marianne Mader employed her knowledge and experience to research historical medical practices for the investigation of the miraculous healing of Sister Mary Theodosia Mug.

- Dr. Avv. Andrea Ambrosi of Rome, postulator of Mother Theodore's Cause, always believed that Mother Theodore – someday – would be recognized as a saint.

And of course, Mother Theodore Guerin, who devoted so many hours to writing letters and journals. The book would not have been possible without her daily contributions ... both past and present. Thank you, Mother Theodore.